# THE HIDDEN WORLD

Number 7

## Beyond the Verge
## Formula from the Underworld
## The Red Legion
## & MORE!

# The Shaver Mystery

## Global Communications

# THE HIDDEN WORLD
## *Number 7*
# THE SHAVER MYSTERY

**Richard S. Shaver**
Ray Palmer
Dewitt C. Chipman
Timothy Green Beckley

This revised edition and new cover art
Copyright © 2010
Timothy Green Beckley
DBA Global Communications, All Rights Reserved

Originally Published by Palmer Publications, Summer 1962 A-6

No part of this book may be reproduced, stored in retrieval system or transmitted in any form or by any means, electronic, mechanical, photocopying, recording, without express permission of the publisher.

Timothy Green Beckley: Editorial
Director Carol Rodriguez: Publishers
Assistant Sean Casteel: Associate Editor
William Kern: Editorial Assistant
Cover Art: Tim Swartz

Printed in the United States of
America For free catalog write:
Global Communications
P.O. Box 753
New Brunswick, NJ 08903

Free Subscription to Conspiracy Journal E-Mail
Newsletter www.conspiracyjournal.com

Note: The four digit numbers at the bottom of each page indicates page number of the entire *The Hidden World* series. Below that is the page number of this book.

THE TRUE STORY OF THE SHAVER & INNER EARTH MYSTERIES

# The HIDDEN WORLD No. 7

**TWO SHOCKING STORIES BY RICHARD SHAVER...**
FORMULA FROM THE UNDERGROUND - THE WOMB OF TANIT
AND...
THE RED LEGION - STRUGGLE OF NATIVE AMERICANS IN THE CAVERNS

An Ongoing Series - This Issue Contains:

JOURNEY THROUGH THE CAVES - HOME OF THE TEN LOST TRIBES OF ISRAEL

Special Introduction by Timothy Green Beckley

Since 1943 the complete realities of the Shaver and other Inner Earth Mysteries have been withheld; now here IS THE WHOLE TRUTH AT LAST - AND NOTHING BUT THE TRUTH - IN THIS REPRINT OF A RARE COLLECTION.

# THE WORLD THAT EXISTS BELOW
## by Timothy Green Beckley

I have been reading stories by Richard Shaver for many a blue, hollow earth moon.

In fact, at the age of 14 I was already a fan of Shaver's. Otherwise, why would I have written my first book on the subject of Shaver and his demented dero? Gray Barker published my initial humble work. *The Shaver Mystery and the Inner Earth* is still in print as *Subterranean Worlds Inside Earth*. The book has gone into so many printings, I can't remember exactly how many. Furthermore, it has been translated into a number of foreign languages (Korean and Japanese at least). Just like UFOs, which Shaver wrote about, the idea of a subsurface world never goes away.

*Hidden World No. 7* is a very interesting edition. It contains two of Richard's longer extrapolations. They both border on the edge of incredibility. They are mesmerizing. They suck in your soul. They have not seen the light of printers ink in over 40 years, so collectors will get an additional adrenalin rush out of reading these.

I really get a kick out of Ray Palmer's editorial. You never know where he is going to go with his assertions. There always seems to be something holding him back from getting the issue out on time. He never quite says the Dero are tampering with the presses, but its sort of implied.

The conclusion of the article on the "Lost Tribes of Israel" which began in the previous edition is a phenomenon contribution to the subject. The Hidden World series has some really great material to offer. We have nine volumes left to publish. It may take us a while to get them out there into the market but we are determined to get them into the hands of those who NEED TO KNOW what Shaver had to offer.

It's a lot of material, but its well worth the effort to bring it all back in print, believe you me.

Tim Beckley
www.ConspiracyJournal.com

# THE HIDDEN WORLD

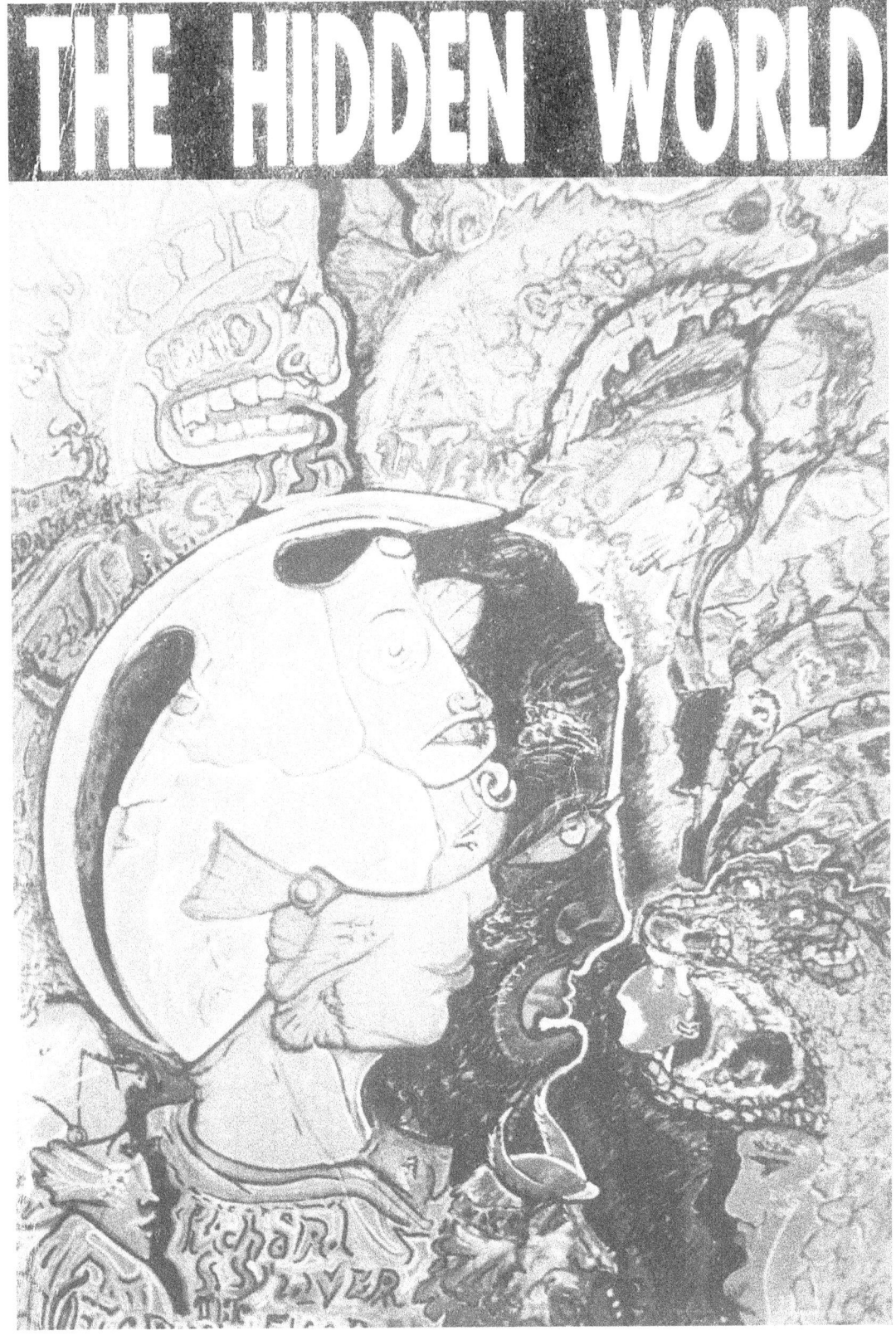

# THE HIDDEN WORLD

# The HIDDEN WORLD

ISSUE NO. A-7
FALL, 1962

## Contents

EDITORIAL . . . . . . . . . . . 1150
    Ray Palmer
BEYOND THE VERGE . . . 1154
    (CONCLUSION)
    DeWitt C. Chipman
FORMULA FROM
    THE UNDERWORLD . . 1214
    Richard S. Shaver
THE RED LEGION . . . . . 1254
    Richard S. Shaver
LETTERS . . . . . . . . . . . . 1337
    From Our Readers

Cover painting by
Richard S. Shaver

---

Address all correspondence to THE HIDDEN WORLD, Amherst, Wisconsin.

THE HIDDEN WORLD is published quarterly by Palmer Publications, Inc., C-137 Hickory, Mundelein, Illinois. Reentered as second class matter at the Post Office at Amherst, Wisconsin. Manuscripts, artwork, photographs invited, but no responsibility is undertaken for loss. No payment is made except by arrangement. Return envelope and postage necessary to insure return. Subscriptions, 4 issues for $6.00; 8 issues for $12.00; 12 issues for $18.00. Some material in this issue is copyrighted and may not be reproduced without the permission of the copyright owner.

# EDITORIAL

## By Ray Palmer

DUE TO THE FACT that the Summer issue of THE HIDDEN WORLD was so very late, we are publishing the Fall issue immediately after the Summer issue, thus almost making it "on time". With the Winter issue, we will be back on schedule. Perhaps it would be asking too much to expect that there would be no hitches in the publication of the amazing "behind the scenes" information on The Shaver Mystery. It never has gone smoothly in all the years since 1943 - why expect it to happen now?

In this issue we had to make compromises, inserting material we hadn't planned on, and holding back more vitally interesting matter, simply because it was the only way to hasten the return to a regular schedule. The material we intend to present takes an enormous amount of work to prepare. It will tax this editor's time and ingenuity to the extreme. But it will be worth it. Imagine a half-million words of "Indian talk" to be straightened out into readable English - and a file of private correspondence between your editor and Mr. Shaver in which he detailed the facts behind all his fiction, as it was being written. It is here that we will sift the fiction out of the fact, and broaden your understanding in the same manner as that of your editor was broadened. At the same time, you will find that these personal letters are some of the best proof obtainable of the absolute sincerity and truthfulness of Mr. Shaver in presenting his account to the editor of a fiction magazine - the only listener he could find!

Included in this issue are two of the more important of

RICHARD S. SHAVER

the stories of Mr. Shaver, in that they detail much of the lore of the caverns in graphic form. Also, the story of the Red Legion will serve to point up the importance of the psychic writing by an Indian who lived 10,000 years ago and saw the Grand Canyon formed! Think of it - Shaver was saying in his story the things that a psychic was saying by automatic writing. The amazing dovetailing will leave you gasping, and ought to confound any experts, if any are still around after these seven issues of THE HIDDEN WORLD.

One thing we want to do, at least partially, in this issue is to keep a promise made in the last issue - to present a picture of Mr. Shaver and also of your editor. We won't be able to present the biographies this time, but we will in a future issue. Meanwhile, gaze upon the two pictures, and be certain that these are two individual persons, and not your editor writing under two names! We often wonder why it is that so many are so certain no Mr. Shaver exists? But if you still doubt, perhaps we can produce legal proof. It shouldn't be necessary, though.

As you look at the photo of Shaver, remember that it was taken about nine years ago on his farm. At the time he was seated on his tractor, and was leading the life of a happy, though amazingly inexperienced farmer. That is why he does not farm today. But he is still as jovial as you see him in this picture - and if this is the picture of a "nut", then all of you are nuts! Don't you agree?

The photo of your editor was taken in 1945 when the Shaver Mystery first began. He is older now, and not a bit smarter. If he were actually smart, he would forget the whole Shaver Mystery, because of the trouble it has caused him in the past. Trouble that seems not to end. It is the most amazing coincidence that not once in 17 years has any activity in trying to present the facts behind the Shaver Mystery failed to bring a string of events that seem as though they were directed by the very Devil himself!

Bender was frightened off by his three men in black. Your editor has had experiences which included no men in black, but just as terrifying. Facing seeming attempts on your life, time after time, adds up finally to the suspicion that you have a persecution complex - and that is where you leave it, because it is much better to believe that is what it is - and it is!

Yesterday we leafed through some of the Shaver file, and were startled to find a half-dozen pages half-burned! They were charred black, and 50% unreadable. Hasty perusal

RAY PALMER

showed that this was a particularly informative bit of writing, and now it was almost impossible to reproduce. Yet the pages before and after it were not even scorched! How do you face a thing like that? Fortunately YOU don't have to!

THE HIDDEN WORLD

HOME OF THE TEN LOST TRIBES OF ISRAEL

By

DE WITT C. CHIPMAN

The initial portion of this novel appeared
in the Spring, 1962 issue of THE HIDDEN
WORLD. This is the concluding installment

## CHAPTER XXI.

## THE JOURNEY THROUGH THE CAVE.

EARLY in the morning, being fully equipped, they started, with candles blazing, and soon left the light of day behind them, and followed the channel into the dark hole in the mountain.

Although intensely dark, with two candles, and walking side by side, they had no difficulty in proceeding with their journey. They encountered many windings and turnings. The way was wide, and as unobstructed as it was out in the day, until they came to a place impeded by a huge fallen rock which so nearly closed the way that they had to go on their hands and knees to get through. At this moment Nardo called a halt, and tied a small rope around his body, and the other end to Iran. Thus guarded Iran went ahead some twenty feet, and after crawling for a short time, he cried out, "Hold tight, the road goes down perpendicular, and I am looking into a dark, black pit. It is so deep that the light can't reach the bottom." This was startling news.

They were silent for a time, when Nardo said, "Throw a stone and listen."

Iran picked up a small stone, threw it into the pit, and in a second or two a ping told that it had reached the bottom. He threw another with the same result. He tied a stone to a small rope, let it down, and presently it struck the bottom. He tossed and swung it round with a like result. The rope-ladder was let down, and Iran descended with a light to the bottom, and said:

"It is solid here; it's all right, like what we have seen already. It is smooth and nice."

Nardo then descended. They left the rope-ladder, so they could get back when they wanted to, and then traveled on. After seven hours, during which they computed they had traveled fifteen miles, they saw a speck of light. In a quarter of an hour they emerged out into the daylight, and beheld a new and unknown country. They were high up on the mountain's side. Rolling hills, covered with dense timber lay below them, and beyond the hills, woods, prairie, and beyond the prairie, a vast expanse of water dotted the islands.

To the left spread a broad country of prairie, woods, rolling bluffs; and flocks of elk, deer, and buffaloes, and other animals could just be seen. To the extreme right, far away, the deep sound of water was heard; a vast mist arose, blocking the entire sky, and Nardo knew from the description, that far beyond the mist lay the Happy Isle, where Rebecca was living. He turned, gazed long and steadfastly in that direction, heaved a deep sigh, and said to himself:

"One year - Rebecca - the Mirror of God."

Then with a high resolve shining on his face, he brushed aside his melancholy emotions, and said to Iran:

"Where deer, elk, and buffaloes are, wolves, wild-cats, and panthers abound. Night is near, gather wood for a fire; we will build it in front of the mouth of the tunnel, and spend the night in there."

Nardo returned to the mouth, while Iran gathered dry limbs enough to last through the night, and after eating supper they lay down for sleep.

During the night they heard the scream of a panther, the yowl of a wild-cat, the howl of wolves, and the hooting of owls.

Their fire was a good protection. The hours wore away, and when morning came they prepared for the events of the day which are related in the next chapter.

## CHAPTER XXII.

### THE DAY'S ADVENTURE.

AFTER breakfast Nardo gazed long out over the hills, woods, prairie, waters, and countless islands, which extended beyond his sight. In the far distance the skies came down, meeting the earth, and they seemed to blend in one.

After having made up his mind what to do, he turned to Iran and said: "I see nowhere any evidence of inhabitants. This is surely the breeding-place of those numerous droves of animals, birds, and fish that swarm from some unknown country from the north, and cover the exterior world. We must return to our tent, get our spears, balls of fire, trumpet, drum, cots, ropes, and other needed things, and bring them all here, as I intend to spend most of the year in this country, to thoroughly explore this land, and we will need all to protect ourselves among those swarming animals;" and he pointed out beyond the woods to the prairie, all dotted over with animals as far as they could see. "You will recollect, Iran, that nothing but the trumpet and drum frightened the wild hogs, and all animals except the pec-

## THE HIDDEN WORLD

caries. The time may come on these prairies, in these woods and on those distant islands, when we may need them more than spears or our fire-balls."

And so, putting their things in a safe place, with their candles and short swords they returned to their tent, and in a week they transported all they wanted to the mouth of the cave. They built a high platform up beside the precipitous rocks for their things, and prepared themselves for the next day, when they would start out on their explorations. They slept on this high platform, and during the night they heard wolves devouring a deer not more than a few hundred feet from them. They shouted to drive the wolves away; but, instead of leaving, the wolves advanced in a body close under their platform, and they could see their shining eyes looking up at them. Nardo shot one; Iran threw down a ball of fire. They scattered from the fire, but after it had died out they gathered again; their upturned heads and glowing eyes were shining as fierce as ever. Nardo thought of the drum. He silently pointed at it, and Iran beat it furiously. At its first sound all the wolves squatted and looked up. At this moment Nardo blew a sudden and loud blast upon the trumpet. The effect was electrical and instantaneous. As moved by one common fear, they all fled, and soon not a wolf remained, nor were they troubled any more by them that night.

No one has been able to explain it, but the hunters of elephants and tigers drive them into corrals, or before the hunters, with drums, horns, bugles, and trumpets; and Nardo was well pleased with this experiment, as he felt that, with trumpet and drum, they could proceed with comparative safety.

The next day, with trumpet, drum, spears, bows, arrows, cots, ropes, and cords, they descended the mountain-side, passed through the woods, and emerged upon the open prairie, where deer, elk, buffaloes, and prairie-chickens could be seen in every direction. They traveled through this wonderful country all day. They selected a solitary tree before night, so far away from any other one that no wild-cat or panther could spring from another tree to them. Near the close of the day they hung their hammocks

1157

## THE HIDDEN WORLD

high above the ground, and after supper, as twilight approached, ascended the rope-ladder, and with a sense of security, resigned themselves to repose. Weary with the toils of the day, they were soon asleep. Once or twice in the night they awoke, heard deer and elk go by, caught the light of the eyes of wolves; but, high up out of reach, they felt no fear, and peacefully sank to sleep until the dawn of day.

When morning came they sat up, and spent an hour in looking around. Birds were winging their way, singing and flitting here and there; flocks of deer were feeding quietly. At every flock was a buck, with spreading horns, standing guard on higher ground than the feeding flock, turning his head in all directions, moving his ears back and forth, occasionally sticking his nose out straight and sniffing the breeze suspiciously; then, being reassured, drew up his head again and resumed his watchfulness. In the nearest flock there was a large, stately animal, the finest in sight, and he was so near that from their elevated station they could see all that was going on.

While Nardo was admiring the stately animal, his grace and knightly bearing, his ceaseless watchfulness, Iran touched his arm, pointed toward a low swail which partly encircled the flock, and he saw something which commanded all his attention. Out of sight of the deer, and lying prone on the ground, was a gang of wolves. They had approached as near as they could without being seen or smelled.

With a silent motion, Iran pointed to the softly-waving grass, and said in a low whisper: "See, the cunning wolves are on the leeward side of the wind."

It was indeed so. The wind was blowing from the deer towards the wolves. The deer could not scent the wolves, but it was evident by their action that they had the scent of the deer, and were planning to circumvent them.

One old shaggy patriarch of a wolf arose, trotted along the swail, rose over the swell, and continued along leisurely in sight of the sentinel buck. In a course which took him quarterly away from the flock, he trotted on, as if on a journey, and he had no designs upon him or his charge. Hard-

1158

ly had his shaggy form risen over the swell than the buck sighted his foe, and faced instantly towards him. Stamping the ground, he blew a signal of alarm. Every head of the feeding flock came up with a jerk; each looked wildly around. Seeing the direction the sentinel was gazing, they all saw the wolf, and hastened towards the buck's side, and, with glowing eyes and dilated nostrils, gazed upon their mortal foe. They all looked at the wolf until he trotted over and down a rise out of sight.

No sooner had the wolf gotten fairly out of sight than he whirled sharp to the right, ran with all his might until he was exactly back and opposite to the deer and lurking wolves; he then, dropping to the ground, crawled up the rise, and with his head concealed in the grass he looked slyly at the deer. The buck, with head up, was gazing towards the point where the wolf had disappeared.

Nardo spoke low and said, "Iran, go down and get breakfast while I watch these wolves and deer, and yonder buck."

After many minutes in silent gazing, first on one and then another, the deer dropped their heads, nipped a mouthful of grass, and while eating it gazed towards where the wolf was last seen. And while eating their long ears played back and forth, turning in various directions, while nostrils and eyes kept guard of that life which was in constant peril. Meanwhile the old wolf crawled forwards in the grass and stealthily approached the feeding deer, who were gradually spreading out and away, step by step, from the sentinel. It would have been impossible for the keenest vision to have seen the creeping wolf unless one had been looking steadfastly in that direction, for he lay flat on the ground, and the grass hid him from sight. And he did not often raise his head above the grass; when he did, he was head on towards the deer. Nothing but his ears and nose could be seen, and their immediate withdrawal would leave one in doubt if it had been observed. It was the evident intention of the wolf to get near enough to spring and catch a deer, and to stampede the balance to the lurking wolves behind the hill. In this insidious manner the wolf was gradually drawing near. It seemed that he would be successful. Nardo was in the act of putting the trumpet to his mouth to blow a blast, when the buck snorted, jumped up and down on the ground, faced towards the creeping wolf, and, stamping his foot, whistled shrilly, for he had scented on the breeze what his vigilant eyes had failed to discover.

Instantly the other deer started on a run to the leader, who, with his white flag up, bounded swiftly away, followed by all the herd. The wolf, seeing he was discovered, gave a savage cry, and bounding from the ground started for the deer, attempting to drive them into the jaws of the pack concealed in the grass over the swell. It is the habit of deer when first started to bound to some higher ground if near, pause a moment to look at the danger, then to dash away and run for life. And in doing this the old buck had partly passed the woves in ambuscade. When they heard the cry of the old wolf they understood what it meant; by common impulse they dashed out of the grass and up the rise where they supposed the deer would be. But they were mistaken, as the deer were running wildly quarterly away, and soon a furious chase ensued. After the first flurry the deer made directly towards a herd of buffalo, who were in loose order feeding, but as soon as they saw the wolves they gathered into a huddle, making a cordon of bowed heads and horns, and stopped the onset of the wolves; the deer ran through the buffaloes before they gathered, disappeared over a rise, and were safe from their enemies. The wolves gave up the chase; gradually the buffaloes dispersed and commenced feeding again.

Iran called Nardo to breakfast. Soon men, buffaloes, and wolves were engaged alike in partaking of food. When their meal was finished, they ascended the tree, beat the drum, and sounded the trumpet. Wolves and buffaloes raised their heads, listened for a few seconds to the rumbling drum and blaring trumpet, and then hurried away. Soon nothing could be seen by Nardo and Iran but the prairie grass and flowers waving in the gentle morning breeze; all was peaceful and still, as a few moments before it had been full of active life and savage violence.

1160

## THE HIDDEN WORLD

We find that a detailed description of the discoveries of Nardo and Iran would extend our narrative much beyond our purpose, and we must merely mention some of them, leaving the reader's imagination to supply the balance.

Their journey extended over a thousand miles. In one part of their trip they found a sea with fifteen hundred islands. It was where the ducks and geese had their breeding-place. Islands rose precipitously from the water some fifty feet, so that no animals could swim from the mainland and climb up. On the interior of these islands were thousands of lakes with extensive marshes, rushes, grass plots, and among these the ducks and geese raised their young. But they occupied different islands, and thus perfect peace reigned, so essential to raising broods.

At another place they encountered a range of mountains rising peak above peak, and on the different peaks, which were often miles apart, and on each ridge or range, the eagles, vultures, and owls were bred; and on lower ridges smaller birds, squirrels, rabbits, foxes, and below them bears, wolves, and wolverines. And on the broad pampas and extended plains, buffalo, deer, elk, antelopes, and musk-oxen were bred. And they noticed that the food and climatic conditions appropriate to each life were abundantly supplied.

Any one can see that these animals could not be bred among men, but only in this country, separated from man by the ice and snow of the arctic zone. On the outside of the verge they would not disturb man, and safe and secure from each other in the place God designed for them, supplied by abundant food, and protected by climatic influences, and by a proper position of land, prairie, woods, swamps, rivers, lakes, inland lagoons, marshes, islands, seas, winding bays, and archipelagoes, and all shut out from any intrusion or destruction of man, especially provided for by an all-wise and omnipotent Mind, these multitudes could be propagated, and sent by an instinct to swarm out, migrate back and forth, for the use of man, and for their own protection and continuous reproduction.

In this land, between an arctic climate without, and a torrid one within, they obeyed the law of nature to produce

1161

their own kind. Here they bred, undisturbed by man, and in pursuance of a law written in their being by the finger of Omnipotence.

Nardo and Iran are the only persons who ever penetrated this land, as it is surrounded, as the reader sees, by inaccessible mountains on three sides, and a frozen sea on the other, which has hitherto marked the boundaries of man's dominion.

It was only by following the pointing finger of the Old Man along the precipice, and the dark tunnel through the mountain, that these two persons ever penetrated into the secluded and mysterious breeding-place of Nature. Ever since man has had a tradition or history, the migration of animals and birds has been known; but an impenetrable mystery has hung like a veil, behind which only Nardo and Iran have ever seen. As the reader knows, deep within the interior, it never rains, but the thunder-storm witnessed by Nardo was along that zone bordering between the interior and exterior worlds.

No doubt many readers will scoff at the idea of a rainless world as much as they will at this breeding-place of animal life, but such incredulous persons will, no doubt, recall the fact that there are many places on our earth where it never rains.

At the end of ten months after the sailing away of Rebecca, Nardo and Iran climbed up the side of the mountains to the mouth of the cave to return to their old camping-ground, there to await the time when the White Ship should come, and the annual test occur before the Mirror of God.

They found the mouth of the cave, and proceeded to where the rope hung over the perpendicular descent, and there camped for the night, to resume the journey in the morning, hoping once more to be back to their old tent, on the margin of the cold and hot water stream.

# THE HIDDEN WORLD
## CHAPTER XXIII.

### THE OLD MAN AND NARDO.

DURING the night Nardo suddenly awoke, and a soft, beautiful, and brilliant light shone around him. The rope-ladder, the perpendicular descent, and the whole interior shone like silver. Iran was fast asleep, and seemed undisturbed, but there, standing before him, was the Old Man he and Melchisedec, had seen, and the one who had given Iran the light and pointed the way along the precipice, to the spot where they now stood face to face. Although surprised and speechless with amazement, Nardo was not alarmed, for he who has made peace with God feels no fear anywhere, for he knows God will always protect those who are in real covenant relations with Him.

He recalled the earthquake, the wonderful crossing of the river, Iran's light, his rescue from the boiling waters, and felt sure that the presence of the Old Man boded no evil to him, but something for his good. Looking intently he found the Old Man was not old in fact. His hair was white as the driven snow, his beard like the one of ancient days; there were no wrinkles on his face, his forehead was as white as Parian marble, his cheeks round and full, his eyes of wonderful brightness, shining with mingled intelligence, abounding benevolence, and childlike tenderness. It was a face to inspire reverence, respect, admiration, and unshaken confidence. Before he spoke Nardo was perfectly self-possessed, but quite curious to know his mission.

"Mortal," and his voice was sweet and melodious, "your spirit is tranquil, your heart pure, your faith sound, your future promising, but I have something to say to you personally; follow me a short distance and let your servant sleep."

Without any hesitation Nardo arose and followed the strange visitor. They proceeded but a short distance, when they turned into an opening that Nardo had not noticed before, and soon entered a large round room in shape much like the rotunda at the capitol at Washington, D.C., but immensely larger. In the center were two alabaster chairs. Taking one, he motioned Nardo to the other, and then the Old Man spoke and said:

"Mortal, I have been congnizant of all your doings since the wandering Christian missionary brought you into covenant relation with Christ, as detailed to the Jewish maiden, Rebecca, and I have been your protector for years, your unseen guide, but this is our first interview, and when you go to the Happy Isle, one greater than Melchisedec or a Mahatma will be your protector.

Having travelled the path of life more than three thousand years ago, I can speak from personal experience, and a few words of wisdom will do no harm, for they will enable you to see the grandeur of life and the beauty and holiness of the Lord.

"I feel certain, reverend Rabbi," said Nardo, "that whatever you may say will be treasured until death."

"Stop, mortal, say not 'death.' There is no death. Only a change. The spirit of man is immortal. All have lived before - a change only occurs as we shake off the flesh and the spirit steps out, and will continue to live for evermore. Had Adam been created he would have had a beginning, and a beginning implies an ending. Immortality never had a beginning, and so will never have an ending. You will never die. I call you mortal, but it is a misnomer. The term mortal covers the time you are in the flesh, but has no meaning when it relates to the spirit after its resurrection, for that will never die, but will pass through endless changes and conditions forever. There is no real abiding substance, only the spirit is real, and unchangeable and indestructible. The clouds are always changing; the sky is not a permanency. It is blue, gray, white, dark, and overcast with clouds, misty with rain, blustering with snow, flashing with lightning, booming with thunder, or radiant with sunshine, but ever-changing and evanescent. The waters change by cold or heat into frost, ice, or snow, and if boiled, turn into vapor and disappear. God could by changing the elements turn the air into fire, heat the river, oceans and lakes, and all would be turned into vapor, into invisible gas, into spirit,

1164

and reduce all to the real substance, spirit, and spirit is God, and that is the limit of human knowledge. The solid rocks, the soils, the minerals, can likewise be so changed. Chemistry teaches us that all can be resolved into elemental substance. You therefore discover what we call matter is illusive and not real. The globe in the hands of God is but a bubble. You see, therefore, He can make an inner and an outer world, and it will float as light in His hand as a soap-bubble in the air. For purposes which suit Him, He has put life into vegetables, plants, grain, animals, fish, and birds, and man has been given dominion over all. He is placed at the head of creation, with dominion over all. He never intended man to labor, but put him as an overseer into His garden - the world. But man chose evil rather than good, and by an immutable law he must take the consequences of his act.

" 'Whatsoever ye sow that also shall ye reap.' That is the one fundamental idea I desire you to remember. Ben Husa sowed in wrath, and met his reward. Ten Osta, the Alatonga, and the brother of Ten Osta, are examples you have witnessed, and the giving way to wrath darkened your spirit, clouded your hearing and Rebecca sailed away alone and disconsolate in the White Ship. In a short time you will stand before the Mirror of God. Before standing this test, turn your mental eye in on your heart, and see if it is as clean and pure as the mercy-seat in the Holy of Holies. You should know that man's heart is God's abiding-place. Out of it should be burned every impure thought. As man's heart is so is the man. Measured by this unfailing talisman, each person can turn the eye of the spirit in on his own heart, and he can know of a certainty just how he stands in the eye of God. Man can be his own judge. The barometer, while in cloud and mist and cold, yet feels and proclaims the coming sunshine. And so in a time of grief and sorrow, hope can throw across the darkest hour a gleam of the coming glory.

"You are a born Chickimec, by adoption a Jew, and let me tell you, while the Jewish religion is true in announcing to the world that there is but one God, it is not the broad religion of Christ, because it is a tribal religion, limited to

1165

the descendants of Abraham, and teaching us that God repents, that He gets angry and passionate; in a word, He has the passions and frailties of man. It believes in sanitary measures, purification by water, not by the spirit, a religion that believes in types and shadows, and is full of ceremonies.

"Christ taught no creeds, He had no ceremonies, He cast out error, He taught purity of heart and spirit, He taught to save all mankind, and as the sunshine is for all, so Christ took in Sadducees, Essenes, Pharisees, Jews, and Gentiles. Jesus said, 'If any one keep My word, he will never die.'

"Life is but a dream. Men are dreamers all their lives, and they awake from the dream of death with bodies invisible to the living. Deserted by the spirit the body decays, and the matter of which it is composed dissolves into the element from whence it came, and the spirit returns to God, who gave it. Jesus came to heal the sick, giving sight to the blind, to raise the dead, and thus prove Himself divine. He came to destroy death and purify the heart. He came not to destroy man, but to fulfill the prophecies. The spirit of man, naturally, is pure and perfect, but clouded by sickness and the flesh. The woman of old had the right conception of the matter when she said, "I've gotten a man of God.'

"When you have lived as long as I have, you will learn that 'the mind sees, hears, feels, and speaks.' Matter of itself, not connected with mind, cannot see, feel, or think. There is no doubt but when we have a comprehension of life and spirit we come as near solving the problem of immortality as is possible for man. You wonder who and what I am. The world calls me a Mahatma. As they attempt to describe us, they say a Mahatma is a man who has studied matter and mind until he has found that matter is not substance, only a condition; and by a wonderful application of mind he becomes capable of composing and recomposing matter, or in other words, compounding and controlling matter, to vaporize it, and then make it do his bidding. The light you see here and the light you saw shining when you awoke is what men call electricity. Science can evolve it

1166

out of matter. The time is coming when man can bring electricity out of all matter, and take pictures with it dispensing with sunlight altogether.* (*Photographer McKee, of Anderson, Indiana, does make photographs by electricity, and after night, which by some are considered superior to those taken by sunlight.)

"The great cataract of falling water makes the electricity that lights the Happy Isle, and takes the place of the sun for the under world. And man on the outer world will yet harness this subtile but resistless power. It will supplant everything as a propelling power for machinery, and all things where force is required. Electricity rides in the air, booms in the thunder, flashes in the lightning, floats in the water, sleeps in matter, and comes forth everywhere at the touch of science. When you go to the Happy Isle, if you ever do, study nature, but study God most, and then you will not live in vain."

"Wise man, or Mahatma, if I may so call you, I shall profit by your advice. I rejoice to know that man is immortal. I accept as true all you say about Christ, and in all the world there is but one thing that concerns me - only one thing that casts a shadow over the future of my life. If you can dissipate that cloud and the fear it inspires, my happiness will be complete."

"Mortal, name the matter, and it will be strange if I cannot find the alembic cup to distill and dissipate this cloud lowering over your happiness."

"We are taught to have no idols."

"That is the teaching of the Scriptures; but it is proper to qualify that by the counter statement that they shall not be put before God."

"Yes; but suppose something was so dear, so captivating, that it was the sole inspiration of life?"

"Is that something an object, or an aim, or an idea, that it would stand before your faith or belief in God? Which would you sacrifice, if the alternative was that or God?"

"I should say God, first, should it break my heart to resign the other, for I love God a little the most."

The Mahatma smiled, and said: "Mortal, you cannot con-

1167

ceal from the eyes of wisdom the secret of your heart; and as candor and directness are the highest and divinest qualities, I will help you out by two words - 'Rebecca!' 'Love!' "

"I will not deny it. I would confess it before the Throne of God. Rebecca is my idol. I would die if it were necessary for happiness or protection."

The face of the Mahatma was beautiful as he said: "God is love. He so loved the world that He gave His only Son. Christ so loved the world that He suffered crucifixion. Do you think God would reprove a man for loving a woman, who was made from next Adam's heart, and divinely designed for him. No, my son. Love is all there is of earth or heaven upon which God always smiles. Love Rebecca with all your might, mind, and soul. A man who so loves a woman will do no vile, foolish, or ignoble act. He will be so noble and chivalric as to merit her love. Love is the freemasonry of the soul. It is the tie binding man to God - the ligament between earth and heaven. Male and female made He them, and in a true marriage they are one flesh."

"Oh, wise Mahatma, I thank God that I have met you, and you have convinced me that the love I bear Rebecca is not idolatry. I see now, as I never saw before, a superadded reason for loving God; for, as you say, God is love, and every moment I live I lift my heart to Him, and bless Him for His goodness to me."

"Mortal, this ever-present thankfulness is God's due. For breath, for food, for all His blessings, day by day, we are the recipients and almoners of His gracious and merciful providence, and all for His mighty love for man, who is little lower than angels, and made in the image of God."

"I am not disposed to argue points I am so willing to accept. I am only too glad to have the opinion of a man who is three thousand years old. We are told that the earth shall pass away, the moon turn to blood, and the sun cease to shine. If these things occur, what becomes of mankind?"

"You will remember that John said, as recorded in Rev. 21:1., as follows:

1168

" 'And I saw a new heaven and a new earth: for the first heaven and the first earth were passed away; and there was no more sea.'

"The moon is said to be waterless and airless, and to be a dead planet. I have already said there is no death. It follows there can be no dead planets. The moon is hollow like our earth. The sun has dried up the waters on its surface. But it is inhabited, and the people there are living on the inside, as the people of the Happy Isle are on this planet, we call earth. The sun having performed its office, becomes functus officio, and in the economy of nature will cease to shine, the moon, lighted by the same electricity which prevails here, its light shining out at the poles, will make it look like blood, and this by the dim light reflected out of its polar openings. That will, in the fullness of time, become the condition of the earth and all its inhabitants will be gathered into its interior parts. We all know the earth is growing larger and larger, the waters getting smaller and smaller, that ancient seaports are now far inland, and in some instances fifty to a hundred miles.

"All our prairies were once seas, but have been uplifted, and are now fertile lands, and when in the countless aeons of time there will be 'no more sea' on the outer crust of the world, and the sun has been burned out, then there will be 'a new heaven and a new earth.' 'The gas in the interior of the earth, and the volcanic agencies will spread and expand the earth and enlarge the inner crust, so that all its people will live inside the sphere, and get their light and heat from the electric sun.' You will remember that Moses records that God created light before the sun was, and nothing is impossible with God.

"Midway between the inner and outer crusts of the world, in what is termed the 'mid-plane space,' there are agencies all the time at work, bringing about these results. These spaces are filled with certain hydrogeneous gas, which being much lighter than the atmosphere, escapes through the apertures, and as it comes in contact with the oxygen of the atmosphere would take fire, and occasion those tremendous explosions.* (*S.T., p. 43 and 44.) which sometimes rend the crust of earth, elevate mountains, and cause volcanoes.

"It can readily be seen how the world would expand like a filling balloon, until it would be large enough to hold the inhabitants of earth. When it is remembered that only a narrow part of the earth is now occupied, not more than one-fifth, counting land and water, and that the water is sinking pari passu and with the increase of population, we can in some measure comprehend the mighty trend of events, as 'the mills of God grind slow but sure.' But, brave Chickimec, remember that the prophesies are to be fulfilled, the Children of Israel, are to be hidden until God lifts the veil, then they are to be gathered at Jerusalem. The world is to be shown the truth of the Scriptures in the redemption of His chosen people, the Millennium will come, and righteousness and peace will cover the land as the waters cover the sea.

"You have but one more conflict with obstacles to overcome, and darkness to confuse and bewilder. Remember always to be cool, collected, never lose faith in God, think of the Mirror of God, the light that lies in Rebecca's eyes, and the uncloying pleasure in the land of the Happy Isle. Take no heed concerning Iran. You will **not** see him any more until he meets you at your tent, on the banks of the cool and boiling streams.

"It is not for you to know the rest now. There are three passages that lead out of this room. They all lead to Iran. This may seem mysterious to you, and whether you travel up or down, straight or on a passage uneven, they will lead to him, and when you and Iran meet, in ten days from that, will come the annual test before the Mirror of God. Take these candles, they will lead you along the way. Should the light at any time be extinguished, take this piece of what you would consider a stone, rub it upon some hard substance, and relight your candles.

"Remember all I have said, and now farewell, while you remain here we shall meet no more. Remember! and farewell!"

Instantly the light vanished before Nardo could speak,
**1170**

and he was left in a darkness as profound as when he was in the channel of the boiling stream.

## CHAPTER XXIV.

### NARDO IN THE DARK.

THE transition from light to darkness was so sudden that Nardo instinctively drew back, rubbed his eyes, and stood bewildered and astonished. What did all this mean? Was it real, or a dream? Had he been dreaming, or had this lengthened interview and singular conversation taken place, or was it the figment of a dream or a nightmare?

It seemed real, but mysterious, and he had been told so many things that he had never heard or thought of before, that it must be real; and so he felt himself, pinched his arm and limbs to see if it was really himself, and if awake or asleep. He felt out in the dark to grasp something, but nothing but the air was in his grasp. He bethought himself to speak, and he cried out: "Iran, Iran, are you awake?" But no answer came. Then he said: "Oh, learned Mahatma, is this real, or am I dreaming?" But he received no answer. When he pinched himself he felt the hurt, or thought he did, or dreamed he did, or imagined he did. He arose from his chair and stepped forward to feel for the Mahatma, who was last seen but six feet away. He advanced two or three steps, and not finding him, he stepped back the same number of steps and felt for his chair, but he could not find it. He went around in a circle, feeling for it, but in vain. A wave of wild excitement swept over him, but he recalled the words, "Be cool, collected, and never lose faith in God." He immediately sat down, to think, on the floor of the room. His hands struck the candles; he recollected the talismanic stone. He rubbed it on the floor, and, lo! a light flashed, and he lighted a candle; but, to his surprise, neither chair was to be seen. It threw but a feeble light on the dense darkness. He could see distinctly but a few feet, and beyond that was Stygian darkness and silence.

He remained motionless for a time, and he could hear the beating of his own heart; for there was such utter silence that his heart seemed like a steam-engine throbbing away in his breast.

He put the talismanic stone in his inner pocket, as something too precious to be lost. He marked the picture of the cross with one candle on the floor, and then started through the darkness to find one of the three passages. He traveled a long time, but could not find the side of the room, which, in the light, had seemed only about two or three hundred feet in diameter. But knowing how often sight deceives one, he traveled on, until, finally, a white object on the floor struck his eyes; and who can paint his astonishment to find it was the cross he had made. He had traveled in a circle, and was at the starting point. He sat down and thought: "If I travel in a circle with a light, what will become of me if I strike a passage and it becomes wide enough for me to circle round and round in it?" Lying on the floor around him he discovered pieces of broken rock of different sizes, but not so large but what they could be managed with one hand. This suggested an idea. It seemed heaven inspired. The Cross of Christ had broken the dominion of death and cast a light across the darkness of the grave, and pointed the way to heaven. And in his heart Nardo said: "It shall lead me out of this bewildering gloom."

The crossbar, like the extended arms of Christ, was the inspiration to Nardo now, and out along the way the right hand would have pointed Nardo laid a line of stones in a straight line. He continued in a sitting posture, hitching along as the line was extended, and so he continued, and in a few minutes his light shone on the walls, which rose above him, and faded out in Stygian darkness. Rejoiced at his success, he put out his hand and eagerly touched the rock, which seemed to him almost as if it were a living friend and brother.

Putting his right hand on the wall, and with his left carrying the candle, he started to discover some one of the three passageways leading out. It was but a short distance before he encountered one, for a black space yawned, and his light no longer gleamed along the rocks, but into impenetrable darkness. Again he marked the sign of the cross, the right hand pointing down the new-found passage, and the other back towards the spot where he had last seen the Mahatma. He started down the tunnel, which descended rapidly; and recollecting the fact that he had entered on a level when he left Iran, he returned to the second cross, and starting a line of stones across the tunnel, in a few moments he saw the rocks, and found the tunnel was not over thirty feet wide.

This was reassuring. He then found the wall, and traveled on until he struck another tunnel, and entering it, he discovered it ascended as rapidly as the first one descended; and turning back, he arrived at the mouth, and started across this with his line of stones. He struck the opposite side, and then continued to advance, and after a time struck a tunnel about the width of the one through which he and the Mahatma had traveled when he left Iran. Rejoiced at this, he made another cross, and joyfully entered it, feeling that he would find the passage where Iran had been left, and his anxiety would cease. With rising hopes, he started and walked rapidly, and was encouraged by seeing that the light shone dimly on both walls, showing that the tunnel was narrow. Soon some misgivings came into his mind, as the way rose and fell, and seemed to bend and curve in a strange manner; but he pressed on, and felt assured because the light shone on both sides, and he could travel without keeping either hand on the wall.

After what seemed a long time, he emerged into a larger way, and the same impenetrable darkness was before him. He paused to collect his thoughts, and then remembering that he should have turned to the left, he started gayly on; but who can paint his dismay when he lost sight of all walls, and was surrounded by the same profound silence and darkness. He went on and on, only to meet the same darkness and silence. He traveled until he finally saw something white near his feet, and, lo! he was at the spot where he had made his first cross; and, after all his wanderings, he was at the point he left hours before.

Weary, worn, and disheartened, he sat down and thought the matter all over. He concluded that he should have followed the first tunnel, if it did descend so steeply. The second ascended too much, and as for the third, he believed it ran in a circle, and had brought him back into the rotunda and back to the cross. He was glad, at all events, to be at the cross he had made, although in such a solitude of darkness and silence. Somewhat calmed, and having solved the course of his footsteps in the dark, and recalling the fact that the Mahatma had said that he should meet Iran at his tent, he arose, and following the line of stones, soon encountered the wall; and it was not long before he encountered his second cross, and it seemed as if he had met a friend; and with rising hope he entered the descending tunnel and resolutely held his way, being careful never to lose sight of its right-hand wall.

After hours of steady descent the course was level for a long time, then descended, and alternated and so on until, wearied and worn, and almost famished, he laid down to rest, nearly delirious with thirst.

While thus lying prone, he heard a soft, low, liquid sound, and after listening with ears that were made preternaturally sharp by the long silence, he was sure it was made by water; and nearly famishing with thirst he arose, but wary from the experience he had undergone, he proceeded carefully down a steeper incline than ever, and at the bottom a bright little stream of water was flowing across the path. He rapidly clambered down, and lying on his breast drank deep and long, the most delicious water he ever tasted. He put three stones together to hold his candle, and bathed his hands and face, and felt refreshed. The water murmured as musical and bright, in its dark mountain home, as if it was flowing under the blue of the skies, or the light of the stars, through the flowery garden of some Andalusian maiden. And in his heart Nardo said, "If the water can sing in this Cimmerian darkness, why should not the spirit of man be bright and hopeful?" While dabbling in the water, something touched his hand. He jerked it back quickly, put the candle close to the water, and saw fish swimming through the pool. He was hungry. The fish rose to the surface, swam leisurely along, and then dove. Watching his chance, when a fin broke the water, he made a clutch, and caught a fish, but with a quick twist, it wriggled out of his hand, fell back with a splash in the water, and all the fish, as if by instinct, disappeared. He regretted this, for the pangs of hunger were gnawing him. Suddenly he remembered that his morning meal was in his coat-pocket. He clapped his hand on it, and there it was. He ate a hearty meal, climbed the opposite side of the way, found a level place, said his prayer, laid down, blew out his candle, and soon was fast asleep.

## CHAPTER XXV.

### IN A VOLCANO.

WHEN he awoke he felt refreshed, relighted his candle, drank, washed, partook of some food, and resumed his lonely way. After some hours' journey he heard a sound, faint at first, but swelling as he advanced, becoming a deep, solemn, and continuous noise. growing louder, more impressive, and at a turn in the tunnel a flash of lurid red light was seen afar off, and a buzzing and trembling of the air, which seemed to impart to the solid rocks a vibrant and tremulous motion, as if they felt the influence of some mighty force.

He continued to advance notwithstanding the increasing noise and growing light. Presently the light was so great that both sides, top, and bottom of the tunnel was illumined, while the deep and profound noise grew more portentous. Though deeply impressed he continued to advance, for it was the only course to pursue. Besides, the ominous noise and light had an irresistible attraction. He believed what the Mahatma had told him, and he knew that God was all-powerful, and Christ all-protecting. His was the trusting faith. While in God's hands, who controls all things, the faithful and the trusting are safe. But when he finally advanced through the glowing heat and light, out on to a broad platform, whose floor was of black shining lava, made so by intense heat, and as smooth as glass, and looked down three miles, upon a gulf of fire five miles across, he stood transfixed with astonishment, for he beheld what mortal never before had seen.

He was looking upon the molten matter of a volcano, inside the earth's crust, in what the world would call the Plutonian regions. Vast waves of melted matter rolled out from under the crust of the earth, on the further side, swept with resistless power across the fiery gulf, and rolled under the crust beneath his feet, with an awful majesty, frightful to behold.

He never felt his insignificance so overpoweringly before. A deep, tremulous motion shook the solid rocks above and around him, and it seemed as if that prodigious mass of volcanic matter must crush, by sheer might, the framework of the globe, and sweep mankind to destruction.

All around this awful chasm, three miles above this sea of rolling fire, was a wide platform half a mile wide, and a mile high, and what had been once evidently the crust, reached out over Nardo, three quarters of a mile, and formed a vast lip over him, which narrowed as it went up towards the upper crust of the earth. And the platform on which he stood had evidently been the bed of the volcano ages before, either when the melted matter was higher by three miles than now, or some mighty upheaval of nature had lifted the platform upwards. The channel which he had followed had been the bed of a boiling stream of water through the rock, and the elevation had run dry and left the channel through which he had been traveling. Cold air came sweeping in at this opening, and it was only by standing back from the front of the platform, and in the current of air, that Nardo could endure the heat.

After the first emotions caused by such a spectacle, Nardo noticed that his tunnel turned to the right around a short shoulder, and was still declining, but not at such an angle as to lead down to the awful fire below. He looked at the hour-glass that he always carried, and found it was after six o'clock, and at this moment he discovered a stream of water, far out and overhead, falling into the rolling cauldron, down and out about three miles from him. As soon as the column of water struck the volcanic matter, an awful explosion followed, and dense masses of steam arose. Vast quantities of gas instantly formed, which poured upwards with a hissing noise, towards the top of the crater and passed out of sight.

Clouds of white sulphurous smoke issued in unceasing impetuosity and tremendous power, puff impelling puff, and rolling to prodigious height, exceedingly white, like vast bales of the whitest cotton. Vast quantities of ashes, stone, scoriae, spouted up thousands of feet and fell back with awful sounds; columns of liquid lava boiled up, whirled around, and ran under the shell of the crust, deep red fires glowed, then black stormy clouds swept across, in places hiding the glare of the fire, at other points glowing with a red subdued luster. Then fiery red spots, flashes of forked lightning played through it all, while rumbling, and profoundly deep subterranean noises shook all the air, and the surface of the surrounding earth groaned, quaked, and trembled, as if it would fall into the tempestuous fermenting, fiery fountain. The falling matter meeting and colliding with the ascending matter formed such a furious and devilish compounding, that no human language can describe it.

Nardo saw waves of hot water rise and dash against the side of the gulf. These waters were hurled up a mile high towards him, and he now understood where the torrent of hot water came from, which thundered so impetuously through the boiling stream near his tent.

He had seen all of the displays of titanic power he cared to behold, and fearing that his delay might endanger his safety, he entered the tunnel at the right and started on his journey, and as he did so noticed with alarm that he had forgotten to blow out his second candle, and there was but a short piece of it left. He thought he had noticed that the general trend of his travels had been downwards and through the mountain in the direction of his tent, but now he was going in a wrong direction. But just before the light from the gulf faded out, a turn in the tunnel shut out all the light and he felt assured that he was traveling in the right direction, and it seemed to him as if a few more hours would bring him home or determine his destiny one way or the other.

As he receded from the glare and noise of the terrible gulf, his nerves, which had been at a high tension, felt unstrung, and he was so tired and weak that he lay down. Just before falling asleep, he gathered his senses enough to feel for his talismanic stone, and finding it safe he blew out his light and soon was fast asleep.

## CHAPTER XXVI.

### PERIL IN THE TUNNEL.

THE slow hours rolled away, and when he awoke the hour-glass had run down and he had lost all idea of time.

He had slept with his feet the way he should go. He arose and started, and in a short time he encountered a stream the size of his wrist, boiling out of the rocks and flowing down a steep decline on the side of the tunnel. He refreshed himself with a drink, and followed the little stream down small cascades and falls for some distance, and at the bottom another tunnel entered at the left, coming down a still steeper decline.

He traveled on, but had passed but a little distance when he heard a roar and a hissing, which he recognized with horror as a boiling stream. He knew his mortal peril; he commenced to run when he heard it thunder down the steep decline he had so recently passed, with an awful roar, and while running with all his might, he fell headlong into a pool of cold water, tumbling over a fall about ten feet high. Rising from the water, it flashed like lightning upon him where he was. He sprung out of the water, turned to the left, and started up the cool stream just as the mighty flood of hot water shot over him and past him; some hot particles splashed and a few drops fell on his hands and face, but he rushed up the cool stream, and felt that he was safe and grateful; for he was within an hour of home, and the boiling stream had failed the second time to destroy him. He knew that by morning it would run down and then he could safely go to his tent. With a heart full of thankfulness, he laid himself down on a smooth rock, in a dry place, in a spot where the temperature was agreeable, between the cold and warm, and with a light but anxious heart prepared to pass the night.

After falling asleep, he awoke once or twice during the night, and finding all things right, he listened to the roaring of the hot water stream, and resigned himself to sleep. Finally he awoke, and he knew by the silence and the coldness that the hot stream had run by; and lighting the remainder of his third candle, commenced a cheerful and happy start for his tent. He was hungry, sore, and weak, but cheerful and full of hope, and the thought of meeting the faithful Iran aided to relieve the weariness of the way.

He had been more seriously tested than he expected when the Mahatma told him, but he had remembered his instructions, and he was happy while splashing his weary way along the stream, every step of which took him nearer his tent and Iran. Finally, at a turn of the tunnel he discovered the welcome light, and soon he emerged into the open, and the sight of grass, flowers, green trees, and hearing the song of birds, and a fresh breeze tossing his hair, were sweet compared to that awful gulf in the Plutonian regions of the earth. As he wearily but cheerfully climbed up the bank of the boiling stream, he saw Iran standing on the bank of the cool stream looking anxiously up the valley they had traveled together months before. He called to him, and Iran turned like a flash and ran with extended arms, and clasping the exhausted Nardo, led him towards the tent, and said, "Oh, master, the Old Man said you would come at this very hour, hungry, wet, and weak, but I was not expecting you that way. But you are safe, thank Jehovah, and I have a warm, nice meal ready. Come, master, and eat."

Iran helped him into the tent. He ate a hearty meal, and lay down to rest with feelings of perfect safety, and soon was sleeping the sleep of a brave and pure-hearted man. He

1179

awoke after a refreshing slumber. He could not see why the Mahatma had subjected him to so severe tests. Yet he felt strengthened by the ordeal. One thing was for a long time mysterious: Why should the water fall into the volcano and cause the boiling of the stream only once a day? At length he reasoned it out this way: The attraction of the moon on the outer world heaped the water of the oceans up under it; that caused the water of the under world to flow rapidly out at all openings; then when the moon, as it traveled rapidly, lost its attraction, the waters returned and made a high tide in the under world, and the rising waters rose and poured through some rent in the cone or shell of the volcano, fell, became hot, boiled up, and found the outlet into the channel of the boiling stream. And at low tide the receding water fell and the boiling stream ran dry, and the cold one had the channel all to itself. He could now see the cause of high and low tides. Also, by the revolution of the earth, the falling of the waters behind would throw the lagging wave on the opposite continent, and the refluent waters would then run back, seeking an equilibrium or a common level. Thus the attraction of the moon and the lashing of the waters on the shores of the internal and external worlds kept the waters in constant agitation, and so caused their circulation all over both crusts of the earth, without and within. Nardo now remembered that in ten days the year would end, and the Mirror of God and a meeting with Rebecca was near at hand if he stood the test, and he proposed with high resolve to do so; and he believed that after he had been so often tested during the last year that no mere machinations of man could stand in the way, and, accompanied by the faithful Iran, he set out to face the Mirror of God, which was to decide his and Rebecca's destiny.

Nardo did not have the scientific knowledge concerning the cause of the circulation of the waters on the earth that we have in the year of grace 1894, and to strengthen his reasoning about the hot water stream, we copy from the Anderson Herald the following in its issue of September 27, 1894:

"The marine globe, an apparatus to produce currents

1180

similar to sea currents, consists of a glass or globe, under the interior wall of which are constructed the massive outline of continents and the hollows of sea basins. The bottom of the sea consists of an interior sphere concentric with the one of glass, moving on a vertical axis and worked by gearing. The sea basins are filled with water containing particles of sterine in suspension, which renders all its movements visible. The exterior of the apparatus does not differ much from that of a geographical globe. When the movable globe turns upon itself," says the Cosmopolitan, "the water is seen to start. From both extra-tropical regions it advances along the sea-bottoms toward the equator; there the two currents from the north and from the south meet, and together rise to a plane of the great circle, reaching the surface in a stream that occupies the equatorial belt of the oceans. The waters pour southward and northward of their line of emergence, then almost immediately turn towards the west. They produce in their course all the secondary currents which are formed by the outlines of the shores and shapes of the sea-bottoms. Through the transparent glass one can follow the movements of the liquid mass and get a better idea of sea currents than from the finest maps. For the best specimens of hydrography seem only dead letters compared with these real moving currents, emerging, advancing on the surface, then disappearing in the depths of these miniature oceans, the capacity of which is scarcely more than a few glasses of water.

Every earnest investigator into the phenomena of nature would be surprised at the facts revealed by this simple instrument, and would, perhaps, be disposed to question the value of certain notions of the physics of the globe, which till now he has held without questioning.

This reference to the marine globe will be the last evidence which I shall offer to sustain Nardo's conclusions, or to fortify the many proofs, scientific, historical, physical, and from navigators and explorers touching the hollow earth. And if to what the little marine apparatus discloses, we will remember that the water rising from the inner world to the upper crust of the world, in passing through the mid-planes, encounters the hot interior parts of the earth, and there becomes heated and forms the mighty warm currents which flow across the world, we can begin to get a conception of what this writer comprehends, and which he is willing to publish and leave to time, and the considerate judgment of all fair-minded and intelligent investigators, to condemn or approve. And now we dismiss all else and turn our attention to Nardo, and what happened to him when he finally presented himself for the final test before the Mirror of God.

## CHAPTER XXVII.

### NARDO AND IRAN AT HEBRON.

AS soon as Nardo and Iran arrived at Hebron, the city where the annual test occurred, it caused a great commotion. The fate of Ben Husa had been deplored and condemned as men decided one way or the other. Nardo and Iran had been detained by various hindrances, and four days had been consumed before their arrival, and in three days the time would come for men of his age to test the Mirror of God. As soon as the relatives and friends of Ben Husa learned of the arrival of Nardo, they put their heads together and caused his arrest on the old charge preferred a year ago. Nardo demanded an immediate trial, but the court had adjourned to witness the annual ceremonies and would not convene again until ten days after.

The case was not bailable. In spite of all Nardo and his friends could do, he was committed to prison.

In company with an officer he was locked up. Some distance from Hebron was a cliff, a lofty precipice, it being a part of the great mountain-chain that shut out all from the mighty oceans, mentioned in a former part of this work.

The rock rose perpendicularly a thousand feet in its general trend. The prison was up two hundred and fifty feet on the side of the rock. To approach the foot of the cliff, a way had been made through the timber and fallen stones to the guardhouse; from that a stairway had been cut in a zigzag manner up the face, to a bench, and a cave in the cliff, where the prison was located. At the top a sentry-house had been built across the face of the cave, a stout door opened into the cave, which was one hundred feet deep and forty to fifty feet wide. Through the center of the cave a little stream ran merrily along, and fell out over the perpendicular wall into the valley below.

Originally the stream ran meandering across the cave, but a way had been channeled through the center, leaving the sides dry and fit for prison purposes. At the back of the cave there was a round hole in the roof, not over a foot in diameter, down which the water poured in a direct fall, splashing into a pool, from whence it flowed out and leaped boldly from the precipice. Before reaching the ground so far below, it broke into sheets, then into drops and then as scattered particles, fell like rain below. The light shining through the falling waters formed a beautiful rainbow which arched across the stream.

On one side of the cave, a lip of the rock reached out, and extended over what had undoubtedly been the bed of the little stream referred to; the water having first burst out there and had gradually cut its way back to the present place of the fall. In its slow course it left the receding bed smooth and open to the sky, and made a promenade for the prisoners some twenty feet wide, the whole length of the channel.

At this dizzy height the prisoners could look out and down upon a world from which they were cut off by hundreds of feet of blue air. Whenever an execution was ordered, they were tied head and feet and tossed to certain death over the precipice. In this secure retreat Nardo was now confined.

The charge against him was groundless, but he was without a remedy.

The second day after his confinement Iran appeared with provisions for Nardo, and with a panther's skin for his master to repose on in the daytime, out on the open platform.

The vigilant sentinel unrolled the skin, carefully inspected the same, and placing his finger on the uncouth figure at the top of some rude drawings, said to Iran:

1183

"What does that mean?"

"That," said Iran, "is to represent a singular bird master killed over in the unknown country. I can't draw good; this is the best I can do."

"I should think not, for I can't tell whether it was made for bird, beast, or scarecrow. But what is this? it looks like a waterfall!"

"Oh, that is the blood, don't you see it falling, and how sick the bird is?"

"Yes, I should think so! That bird is ugly enough to be sick all the time. But here, what is this? it looks suspicious. A bow, arrow, and a string attached!"

"That represents the arrow that killed the panther, and just below the bow is the spot where my master's spear hit the panther. And the string represents the chain of events leading up to the killing of that wonderful bird."

"Oh, yes, you sly old Ishmaelite, come along, tell that tale to Baalam, and his long-eared friend. But come, with your pretty bird, and panther's skin, ornamented with your artistic skill," and he was admitted to the cave.

As soon as Iran saw his master, he said: "Oh, master, I have been explaining to the guard these rude drawings on the panther's skin, that I made. He pokes fun at me, but you will understand all about the panther, the bow and the bird."

Nardo was astonished. Evidently, there was some deeper meaning in Iran's pictures and words than there appeared to be on the face. Nardo had no recollection of a bird. Nor did he know that Iran had ever made any pictures on a panther's skin or on any other skin.

The only panther he could recall was the one slain by the peccaries. And the skin of that one had been torn to shreds.

He detected a peculiar meaning in the looks and manner of Iran, and this put him on his guard, and so he spoke cheerfully and as if amused, and said:

"Well, Iran, I must confess it is somewhat difficult to recognize the bird. The panther's skin - it will be many days before we forget that fight - I'm obliged to you for bringing, as it will be soft to repose on during the day."

"I thought so, master." And while Iran was rolling it up,

1184

he put his finger on the bow, but in such a way that the guard could not see, and said: "Here is where your spear went - and here, where my arrow struck - and you remember it was at one o'clock - you remember, at one o'clock?"

"Certainly," said Nardo, on whom the words "one o'clock," created a dawning suspicion in his mind of some hidden and suggestive meaning.

Iran then withdrew. Nardo took the panther's skin, retired to the remotest end of the platform, spread it out, and commenced a critical examination of Iran's pictographic communication, to see what he could make of it. It was not long before he commenced to gather his meaning.

The pretended body of the bird was really the ledge of rocks where he was confined. What represented the head, when closely scanned, was the cave, the eye of the bird was where the water came down through the top, and the sick bird's retching was the stairs leading to the prison, where the bars on the door, though blurred, could be seen, and the simulated blood was the water pouring over the precipice, and the dark spot on the neck of the bird was where the stream flowed out of the cave.

But the most significant thing was the bow, arrow, and string. The arrow pointed directly to the star in the hindquarters of the bird. That was the point to where the arrow was to carry the string. The string was attached to a rope, as seen by the heavier lines. This was what it all meant, as he understood it: Iran was to shoot an arrow at one o'clock at night, with a string attached. He was to catch the string and pull it up, and also the rope; fasten that, and thus escape from confinement. The cunning Iran had put wings, tail, blood-stains; an eye had been added to resemble a bird, and the whole thing had misled the guard, and it had mystified Nardo for a while, but now he felt he had solved Iran's purpose. Nardo was suddenly inspired with hope. He spent the day in admiring Iran's genius and ingenuity. He planned what he would do to throw his enemies in the dark, and his heart beat high and wild as he thought of the Happy Isle and Rebecca.

We now pass over all other matters, and we find Nardo

at midnight at the point indicated by the star, all attention to the slightest sound. A long time elapsed without any sound indicating life in the dark gulf below. His patience was sorely tried as minutes passed into hours. Had he misunderstood Iran? It was a heart-freezing and soul-chilling thought. If Iran did not mean it, why had he taken so much pains with his drawing. If there was no significance in it, why had he said and repeated the words - "At one o'clock?"

While balancing these thoughts in his mind, there came wafting up from the black abyss the low, long hoot of a kasco, a bird that Iran had learned to imitate while they were in the land of the fifteen hundred islands. No one but Iran and himself had ever heard the peculiar call of the kasco. His heart almost stood still. The call was repeated a little louder, and then sunk to a low sound like a dying echo. There could be no mistake - it was Iran. Nardo tossed a little pebble out beyond where he stood. He followed it with two more, then came the sudden whirr as if a kasco had been scared up, and all was still; but both parties understood each other.

Nardo strained his ears for the slightest noise, when something passed over his head, and a line dropped softly across his shoulder. He grasped it. It was a delicate thread. He gladly clung to it. He slowly and carefully commenced to draw it up. Soon it was arrested, and he felt a slight pull downwards, he responded with a corresponding one, and after two or three interchanges of signals, the line at the lower end gave way, and Nardo drew up the line rapidly and cheerfully. Suddenly the line was arrested, he gave way, thinking for some reason Iran desired it. Presently he recommenced but it stopped again at the same place. He repeated this several times, but it always stopped at the same point. He pulled harder, when suddenly the line parted. It evidently had caught in a crevice in the rock and broke, just as he felt sure of success.

He threw down pebbles to Iran, but received no answer. He threw larger ones, but there was no response. Iran evidently, assured of success, had gone away so he would not be suspected, or had been scared away by fear of dis-

1186

covery. He knew and so did Iran, that if discovered, the penalty for aiding an escape was to be hurled headlong from the cliff. All of Nardo's hopes perished in a moment. Daylight would disclose the arrow, the broken line hanging to the face of the cliff, and the rope, perhaps, dangling at the spot where the line broke. All would be discovered, Iran suspected, redoubled vigilance exercised over him, and his escape rendered improbable.

And this was the result of all his hopes, and on being satisfied that no relief could come from Iran, he began to look over the field to see what next to do. The prospect seemed dark, indeed. From a legal standpoint, he knew he would be acquitted on trial. He had been a resident many more years than was required by the decree of the Sanhedrin.

He was an adopted citizen by all the forms of law, and he needed no permit to marry Rebecca or to be tested for the Happy Isle. Court had adjourned, no civil or religious process could give relief. He was powerless, confined, and helpless.

What if he was innocent, the test would be over before it could be established, and another year must pass over before he could hope to see Rebecca. He was irritated, and in spite of the last year's experience, and the Mahatma's instructions, he found his spirit in rebellion.

From his elevated position in the daytime he could see the White Ship resting on the tide. He saw the flashing light from the Mirror of God, shining on the landscape, and playing on the clouds.

People were constantly passing on to the Platform of Test, and going through the Golden Gate, and here he was, an innocent man, caged like a criminal, and held in durance vile. And - saddest thought of all - what would Rebecca think?

This thought was maddening. He was filled with rage, grief, sorrow, indignation, regret; and then recalling what the Mahatma said, he put his hand on his heart and said:

"Peace, troubled heart - oh, sorrowing soul, be tranquil; crucified Christ, come to my relief!"

At this moment an electric shock passed like lightning

through him. He was wonderfully impressed to turn around, and as he did so, lo! the Mahatma was standing, with folded arms; with the old reposeful, moveless and serene tranquillity, and around him the same marvelous light he had seen in the cave that led to the volcano. A gracious, gentle, and sedate smile, shone or rather wreathed his beautiful face; his clear, penetrating gaze, was full of assurance, resourceful; his brow, while as Parian marble, had about it an air of profound, imperative, masterful intelligence.

His presence calmed the troubled spirit of Nardo. It inspired him with hope and courage. They gazed upon each other silently for a short time, and when Nardo felt composed enough to venture on speech, he said:

"Oh, Mahatma, you left me to Cimmerian darkness, but the cross, the volcano, the boiling stream, and now I feel that your presence means light, not darkness; hope, not despair; the Happy Isle, not a prison."

"Mortal, I was with you in the darkness, in the volcano, in the boiling stream. You will be cared for now as then. Look there!" and Nardo saw a long rope that would reach to the bottom of the cliff. "Be patient. Is your spirit tranquil? Do you trust the arm of the Infinite, or quil? The White Ship, Rebecca; but if your heart is right in the sight of God, you are safe. What is the state of your heart and spirit?"

"Oh, Mahatma, my faith is unshaken. I feel that I am mortal. I chafe at my imprisonment; I condemn the practice which holds me here without a speedy trial. I must remain another year. The hour for testing man is over; that of woman is on. Were I free I could not be tested. How can I, a mortal, be tranquil and resigned? I tell you, as I would tell God, that I am not satisfied. You, oh, Mahatma, are immortal, and you know not the pangs of grief and sorrow that wring the heart of one disappointed in love and treated with the rankest injustice."

"Mortal," said the Mahatma, "you have been very frank. I knew your troubled soul. You were tested sufficiently by me. Your and Iran's scheme fell through. I am here to befriend you. Your case is not so bad as you suppose. 'Tis true, the test for men is over, that of women on; but that for

1188

anchorites and hermits comes after women. There is yet a chance for you."

"Oh, Mahatma, I see the rope will let me down, but the officers of the San Hedrin are before the pathway that leads to the Test. They would stop and re-arrest me. I've no chance."

"Mortal, do you think the Mahatma, is not resourceful? In the grove at your feet is the hut of Sedor Elam, the Anchorite. He is to be tested. All the people know it. Melchisedec has been notified. You but personate him. The people will fall back out of respect to Sedor Elam; you pass unquestioned; and if God's all-seeing eye approves, you will pass the Golden Gate, and all will be well."

"Oh, Mahatma, I'm not old. I haven't his dress; I don't look like him. I'm young, he is old; my hair is black as a raven's, his snowy white; my step is light, his slow and trembling."

"Mortal, be patient. Would not a Mahatma know all these things? See there! Pick up and unroll that bundle."

Nardo eagerly grasped and unrolled the bundle, and, lo! a black gown, a hood, a false face, wrinkled and old, a wig of hair white as Sedor Elam's.

"Oh, Mahatma, I see it all. Christ be praised!"

Something like a smile trembled on the Mahatma's face, just as a sunbeam flecks a cloud, but does not shine through, only illumines and whitens for a second, and then fades away; and in an instant the Mahatma, as grave and sententious as ever, said:

"Now, mortal, give me undivided attention; doubt not, question not, command your spirit, purify your heart; you will soon be in the presence of God, before the tribunal of exact justice, from which there is no escape and no concealment. Sedor Elam would tell you there is never a moment in the life of the wicked but what the cloud of evil and hell rises like a mist from their hearts, and it darkens not only each moment of mortal life, but, should they stand before the Mirror of God, they would see devils, imps, and goblins infernal mock and gibber at them all the time from the mirror. These godless people never have the courage to

1189

take the test; their conscience makes them cowards. Sedor Elam would also tell you that in the land of Abaddon the wicked are tormented six days in a week, and on the seventh, or Sabbath day, they are entirely free from pain; that punishment and pain cease on the Sabbath, and it becomes a day of rest. These wicked ones have been Sabbath-breakers all their days, and now they are only too glad to welcome the Sabbath as a day of rest from pain. God ordained the Sabbath as a day of rest, and by a strange irony of fate, in the land of torment they rest on the Sabbath forever. So God's command, to rest on the Sabbath day, is carried out in the land of condign punishment. You will discover it is best to obey the Commandments. While in the wilderness no manna fell on the Sabbath. God rested on the Sabbath; and if He did, how dare man to desecrate the day? And 2,000 yards was a Sabbath day's journey for the Jews. The River Sambatyon ceased to flow on Sunday.

"Because the sun shines, the rain falls, and the wind blows, on Sunday the wicked pursue their Sabbath-breaking in this life and pray for it in the life everlasting. Man should have some respect and some faith in the Father of All. Abraham, Joseph, Daniel, and Moses had faith stronger than a mustard seed, and the captives in Chaldea dared the loss of their arms rather than sing the songs of Zion to mocking heathen. But, my friend, I think you are prepared for the Test now if ever; see there," and he tossed the falsehood and mantle over the precipice, and said:

"Drop the rope, fasten it firmly, put on the false face and wig, go down the rope, dress yourself to personate Sedor Elam, and go boldly to the Test. But before you go, let me give you final instruction and advice. When you descend and are dressed, go to the hut of Sedor Elam. There you will be safe. Through me he has been advised to look out for you and protect you. No one will seek you there. Remain until the test for women is over.

"I will now give you the highest teaching that a Mahatma can give to man. Not but what Mahatmas know more, but it is the limit of man's comprehension. All things are comprised in three things, the inorganic, organic, and spiritual. All

1190

grow out of, or are reducable to, these three. The inorganic is the base, and depends for development on heat and cold. In the mid planes of the earth all matter is in a state of liquefaction, all is hot melted matter, and it is operated upon by air and water. They harden the melted matter and change it to rock, pulverize it to earth, and thus the inorganic is changed into the organic by chemical and physical changes. From the earth organic life gets its being, and plants, grasses, insects, fruits, flesh, animals, flowers, trees, birds, and man are compounded and recompounded, and become organic, coming from the inorganic. From the organic comes the spiritual. God touches the animal in man, breathes into his nostrils the breath of life, and man becomes a living soul; hence the birth of the spiritual, and there man's absolute knowledge stops.

"The Mahatma has a profound knowledge of nature; he has searched the hidden secrets of the inorganic and the organic till he can trace the link from the gas and liquid lava up through all its stages until in man he finds the spiritual. It is the spiritual life in man that leavens, the animal, enlightens the mind, purifies the heart; it is the atmosphere of the soul lifting man up to the plane of his celestial destiny. The animal in man's nature is at enmity with the spiritual. It degrades man, it is a destroyer, while the spiritual lifts man up and ties him to heaven. The Scriptures enunciate a primal and immortal truth when they declare, 'Whatsoever a man soweth that shall he also reap.' If he sows sin and crime he will reap it. If he sows corruption he will reap corruption. If he sows tares he will reap tares. And so on all through the calendar of crime and unbelief. Remember, when you go to the Happy Isle, that you should cultivate the spiritual and intellectual. If not you will die by inches, because the destroying principle, ignorance and sin, will sear the conscience, cloud the soul, and you will drift away to destruction.

"Once get into rapport with spiritual truth and Christ and you secure immortality. A perfect correspondence with spiritual life means eternal life. Man is the crowning work of creation; his power of comprehension shows the magnificence of his being and links him to the Divine. 'He that hath the Son of God hath life; he that hath not the Son of God hath not life.' A man 'may be noble, of grand caliber, enriched by culture, high-toned, virtuous, pure - he may reach the starry heavens or grasp the magnitude of Time and Space. The stars of heaven are not Heaven. Space is not God.' Before man can control matter like a Mahatma he must understand it. Birth, life, growth, decay, death are around him. He cannot understand God because He is infinite, and finite faculties cannot comprehend the infinite.

"God is unapproachable in knowledge, but approachable in His mercy for His creation. Grass grows, has life, but is blind and has no feeling; cattle eat it, get life and strength and feeling, but no spiritual knowledge; man eats the animal, fruits, and vegetables; he has life, feeling, intellect, and spiritual perceptions, and if brought into covenant relations with God, will live forever. When the earthly tabernacle totters to decay, he will be clothed in spiritual and celestial personality. The wind, the lightning, the thunder, yield to intelligence, and are the obedient servants of the Mahatma. Not because he has usurped any of the preorgatives of God, but because God has given to intellect the power to discover and use those things ordained for His creatures. We are wise enough to know that when God created the world it needed a ruler, a teacher who could lead and educate man's spiritual nature and bring man up out of the material into the spiritual, and into covenant relations with God. Hence the necessity of Christ. The Mahatma stands on that proud height, where he catches the light from heaven, and he dares not question the necessity or divinity of Christ. When you go to the Happy Isle make these things your study.

"One thing will be important for you to know concerning force, on telluric matter. There is such a thing as force, which everywhere pervades nature. Men have imagined it to be two forces. They, or it, is in fact one force; which so counterbalance each other as to maintain an equilibrium throughout the universe. One force we call gravitation; the other is called force, by some magnetism, by others

1192

electricity.

"Gravitation we profess to understand, but force is a mystery, and because it is only understood by its Creator.

"Gravitation holds all things to the earth. Yet that law is overcome when the arrow shoots upward, or the balloon mounts into the air. When the force is spent, gravitation brings them back to the earth, and they become inert. Water is a variable element. Gravitation holds it to the earth. Convert it to vapor, confine it, it has then a mighty power.

"Condense it back to water, gravitation returns, the vapor force is overcome, and it then is a harmless and useful element. Thus you see water is the best exponent of the two forces in one element. Water can become snow, ice, frost, vapor, and water again. It flows from the fountain, bubbles from the spring, glitters in the river and lake, rolls in the ocean, floats in mist, whirls in the clouds, laughs at gravitation, and scorns inertia.

"Mind is the center of the greatest force. It is the central or pivotal point, where intellect and spirit meet in superlative force. Man with his muscles, which are the agents of his intellectual and spiritual forces, moulds the machine, casts cannon, makes sword and spear, dominates over the elephant and lion, and by the forces of mind becomes the lord of creation.

"But who can comprehend force, although we think we can gravitation? We see force in the rolling river, hear it in the rush of the tornado, the rumbling thunder, the flashing lightning stroke, in the roaring volcano, and in the crashing earthquake, when the solid crust of the globe is rent asunder. Still we cannot comprehend it.

"The demons, in the days of Christ, recognized His power, were cast out, and ceased to torment mankind. They mumbled, and muttered, tore their victims and disappeared. Christ treated them as imps of the devil, and they all the time denied His divinity, the existence of God, but submitted to His omnipotent power. Be on your guard against all deceits and mystifying hallucinations. Let several persons seat themselves around a table, put their hands on it, remain silent, and the concentrated force from so many

1193

persons and minds will center in the table and completely magnetize it, and it will creak, move, rap. As this electricity leaps to the table, it will move, tilt, respond by raps, tips, to any questions previously agreed upon. If there is one at the table who has large electricity, or who understands this electric force, he will be the medium through which the principal manifestations come. In lifting or moving any ponderable body, the atoms of force start from the brain, traverse along the arms and hands, electrify the table, the force extends to every particle of the wood, and it is put into vibration, and if the electrical force is sufficient to over come the inertia, the table is lifted, moved, tilted, or responds in knocks to some active-minded medium in the the circle. By a strange metempsychosis, which we cannot now understand, the long dormant memory of the persons present is transmitted to the table, and persons are confounded by a disclosure which they thought they alone possessed, and they think there is something mysterious in it. It is after all but the immortality of memory, which had been evoked in this peculiar manner, and the past is recalled. It follows that what we call force is magnetism, electricity, but what that is no one can tell.

"It is clear that what we call force is nearer magnetism and electricity than any other known thing. After all, like mind or thought, it is invisible, intangible, as mysterious as vapor, but acts in accordance with natural laws; it has no spiritual connection further than all things; and in fact, man finds all things in life a mystery, and man cannot comprehend himself. But as I have described it so you can in a measure better understand that gravity and force hold all things in equilibrium. That they act, counteract, and react, that they are the ligaments which hold the planets, worlds, stars, and creation where the Author placed them at creation.

"Attraction and force will explain many phenomena, and when rightly understood will bring them within laws. You thus see matter requires a law to control it. In a like manner, spiritual man needs a controller, hence a conscience, and a Christ.

1194

"I need not enlarge further. Should you go to the Happy Isle, study these laws, and you may hope some time to become a Mahatma.

"Time presses. Sedor Elam awaits you. Fasten the rope and prepare to descend."

Nardo, inspired with hope, fastened the rope, and having done so, he said while in the act of turning:

"It will do, that is - "

He never finished the sentence, for, as he looked, the Mahatma was gone. Search where he would, he could not be seen. He had disappeared as suddenly as he had appeared. From his experience in the cave, he felt that he had seen the last of the Mahatma for that occasion. He therefore addressed himself to escape. He thoroughly examined the rope. He tested its strength. It resembled in fineness the best of silk. It was flexible and stout. At short intervals were balls, large enough so his feet and hands could get a good support. He felt he could safely descend upon it.

He threw his shoes, the arrow and string of Iran over the cliff, faced the rock, put his bare feet on the balls, grasped the rope with both hands, and swung off from the ledge and dangled over the dark abyss. In a few seconds he disappeared from sight, and only silence, vacancy, and darkness prevailed where so recently such words of wisdom had been spoken. Neither the mysterious Mahatma nor unhappy prisoner was to be seen on the lofty ledge of Hebron's prison. Only the panther's skin remained in sight, when the guard came at the usual hour, to tell the perplexed official that he ever had a prisoner. Even the singular rope had disappeared as completely as the vanished prisoner and the wonderful Mahatma.

Late in the day after the women had been tested, the cry was taken up:

"Sedor Elam!"

An old man dressed in a black gown reaching to the ground, with a hood on his head falling below his shoulders, with long venerable beard, white as snow, face wrinkled and sunken, bent with age, walking by the aid of a cane, came slowly towards the gateway leading to the Mirror of God.

1195

Instantly all gave way, as the old man slowly and wearily advanced. Sedor Elam was known, loved, respected, and venerated by all. For years he had lived a life of a hermit, in the little hut, deep in the shade of the cliff, and now was slowly making his way to the Test. Many expressions of good-will greeted him on the way. Offers of assistance were feebly waived aside. When he arrived at the gateway, it was opened wide, the aged patriarch waved his hand in benediction, while he steadily pursued his way.

Just as he arrived at the platform of Test, and while preparing to step on it, he paused, threw off his gown, his hood, his false face and wig, and Nardo was revealed to all. While the lookers on were dumfounded, he mounted the platform, and immediately the Golden Gate swung wide open, as it had a year before for Rebecca. Nardo passed with active steps, the gate swung to, and he passed forever from the sight of friends and foes at Hebron.

A great uproar occurred when Nardo disappeared, and while at its height the real Sedor Elam appeared, but he was not received with the deference and respect they had accorded to Nardo.

As Nardo did not appear among the men, Rebecca, dejected and sad, was in a distant part of the White Ship, nursing her grief and sorrow, and did not see the approach of her lover.

She had been informed of his arrest, imprisonment, and she was gazing sadly at the far-off prison, when Nardo, with eager, active steps, boarded the White Ship, looking anxiously for Rebecca.

It was a little time after he ascended to the ship before he discovered her. He found her gloomy and dejected, for she believed he was still a prisoner on the distant cliff where her sad eyes had rested for days. To Nardo, Rebecca was as lovely as a seraph, and as for Rebecca, when her eyes fell unexpectedly upon her lover, she threw up her hands for a second in surprise, then with a smothered cry she rushed to him and was folded in his arms. She laid her beautiful head upon his manly breast, while floods of tears of joy fell like glittering pearls from her eyes.

1196

THE HIDDEN WORLD
We drop the veil that none may see
The joy that follows agony.
There are sights to angels given,
Too dear for sight this side of heaven.

When the fond heart all full of love,
And bathed in rapture from above,
When love diffused through every part
Overwhelms with joy the human heart.

The White Ship sped away with snowy sails across the sea of silver. In his hour of supremest happiness, a pang of regret swept through Nardo, as he thought of the faithful Iran left in the City of Hebron. He was glad that he threw the line and arrow over the cliff before he descended, so no telltale was left behind to incriminate him. He solaced himself with the hope that when Iran was old enough he should meet him in the Happy Isle.

The Mirror of God, the Golden Gate, faded away in the distance, as some invisible power sped them swiftly away.

Hebron sank forever from sight without a lingering sigh from Nardo. His last glimpse was on the lofty cliff, and the spot where he had been a prisoner, and where he last saw the good Mahatma. And here we close our book; the veil now descends upon Nardo, Rebecca, Melchisedec, and the Children of Israel. Here it will remain until God permits some heroic Joshua to cross the Northern Verge, and travel down its slope to discover this romantic and chosen people hidden in the extremities of the earth, until God calls them back to Jerusalem in fulfillment of all His prophesies.

# THE HIDDEN WORLD
## APPENDIX.

THE late Sherlock Holmes had a dictum which said:

"Eliminate the impossible, and what is left, however improbable, must be the truth."

As the impossible could never happen, we are not inclined to admit the saying of Mr. Holmes, but we believe nothing is impossible with God.

The world has always been curious concerning the lost Tribes of Israel, and some quotations are made from the work of the Rev. Dr. M. Edrehi, entitled "An Historical Account of the Ten Tribes settled beyond the River Sambatyon in the East."

Edrehi was a learned Jew, and his writing has additional interest on that account. It shows that the Jews believe with the Gentile world, that there is an unsolved mystery in connection with these tribes.

These quotations are not given to sustain or overthrow the theory of this book, but as matters of interest to those who have never read his work, I quote as follows:

"Blessed be his Holy Name, for he is the God of gods, the Holy One and true God. He is mighty and powerful, ever mercifully protecting and watching over us, with compassionate eyes, and performing great miracles on our behalf. Though we are captives and strangers dispersed through other countries, yet the Almighty One has never forsaken us, and of this we have abundant proof."

"This work speaks of the miracles which the blessed God wrought in our behalf, and which He still performs every moment for us, and particularly those in favor of the Ten Tribes who exist at the present day."

"The first testimony to prove the existence of the River Sambatyon, is the Targum Ben Oziel, the Chaldee of Johanathan, the son of Oziel, in the Targum on Exodus xxxiv. 10, saying: 'Behold I make a covenant; before all my people I will do marvels, such as have not been done in all the earth, nor in any nation.'"

"Izatus became king a little while after. It is said that some parts of Noah's Ark are still to be seen in this place."

1198

## THE HIDDEN WORLD

"The Lord shall set his hand again, the second time, to recover the remnant of his people, which shall be left from Assyria and from Egypt, from Parthros, from Cush, from Elam, from Shinar, from Hamath and from the Isles of the sea.

"He shall also set up an ensign for the nations, and shall assemble the outcasts of Israel, and gather together the dispersed of Judah from the four corners of the earth."

"Lastly, the prophet affirms that God shall bring back the outcast of Israel, who are concealed in the extremities of the earth."

Pray where are the extremities of the earth, except at the poles?

"But as for the Jews, they are dispersed; but God shall gather them together, from the four corners of the earth. And I will make them one nation, in the land upon the mountains of Israel, and one king shall be king to them all; and they shall be no more two nations, neither shall they be divided into two kingdoms." This was spoken concerning Judah and Ephraim.

"After the ancient Rabbis had made known, or discovered the rotundity of the earth, with the five circles, i.e., the arctic and antarctic circles, the tropics and the equator, and had ascertained the measurement of the globe, they made diligent search for the Ten Tribes and some of them gave up the search, thinking it to be vain."

"Josephus is an author very much esteemed, well known among all nations; and he writes a great deal about the ceremonies of the Ten Tribes, and he mentions that they are at the other side of the River Sambatyon."

"The breadth of the River Sambatyon is full 220 yards; and contains sand and stones; and the noise of these stones makes it like thunder and hurricanes; they rise up and go down, the noise whereof at night may be heard at half a league distance. There are also many springs and fountains of soft water, which empty themselves into a basin, from whence the gardens and orchards are watered. The stones before named which make so much noise, and move up and down, repose from the setting in to the going down of the

1199

Sabbath; and around the river there is a fire descends from heaven every day in the week, and remains there, except Sabbath; so that no person can approach the river, for the fire burns everything within its reach."

"When we came to the city near to Sambatyon, we heard a great noise and roar as a tempest; and the nearer we approached the Sambatyon, the greater the noise."

"All the week the stones are thrown as high as a lofty house; the noise is so great as to be heard at the distance of two days' journey; and on Friday two hours before the Sabbath, they remain undisturbed. The river dries up, the stones disappear, and nothing but very white sand is seen, and on the going out of the Sabbath everything continues as it was before."

"Do you hope for and expect that God will, when His infinite wisdom shall think proper, gather us all from amongst the nations and resettle us in the Holy Land by means of a prince from the house of David, and that the holy temple will be then rebuilt and the kingdom of Israel reestablished?"

"The Lord God will restore you from your captivity, and will have mercy on you, and He will return and collect you together from amongst all nations whither the Lord your God has dispersed you, even if you be driven to the extremities of the heavens; the Lord your God will from thence call you forth and assemble you together, and will convey you to the land which your forefathers possessed, and you shall inherit it, and He will prosper you and make you more numerous than your fathers."

"The prophet Jeremiah likewise assures us in the time when the Lord pleases, that He will save His people, the remnant of Israel; that He will bring them from the north, and gather them from the four corners of the earth, in great bodies, to reestablish them in the Holy Land, for He is a father unto Israel, and Ephraim is His son."

"It is known that nowhere in the Scripture is it asserted or intimated that the Judaical law is the adumbration or figure of any other law; on the contrary, it is everywhere said that the law of Moses is to be eternal."

1200

The prophets predict to the Jews in their calamities that they should be one day delivered, but that their deliverer would be the support and not the destroyer of the Mosaic law.

"A great proof of the verity of the Jewish religion is its immutability. The Jews of Barbary, Turkey, Germany, Poland, England, Holland, France, Italy, India, Persia, China, and every other country have always, since the taking of Jerusalem, by Titus, held the same doctrines; no contradictory sects and no schism distract them, all agree and are in unison; there is no variation in the observance of the Commandments delivered from Mount Sinai. The preservation of the Jewish nation through so many ages, and the total destruction of their enemies, are wonderful by being signified beforehand by the spirit of prophecy. The preservation of the Jewish nation, is a signal and illustrious act of Divine Providence. They are dispersed among all nations, and not confounded with them. The drops of rain that fall, and the great rivers which flow into the ocean, are mingled and lost in that great and immense body of water; and such would have been the fate of the Jewish nation; in the ordinary course of nature, they would have been mingled and lost in the common mass of mankind, but they flow in all parts, blend with all nations, and yet are religiously and civilly separated from all; they still remain in their faith a distinct people, they are unable to live conformable to their laws, they nowhere select their own magistrates, nowhere exercise the whole of their religion, intolerance restrains them; they are checked, bruised, and contemned, yet they are wonderfully saved; they are preserved from oppression like their ancestors, Moses in the bulrushes, or Daniel in the lions' den; human power is frustrated, and there is no destroying whom God chooses to preserve."

The Jews seem everywhere to be a living miracle among nations of the truth of the Bible. And as bearing on the theory of this book I cite the following to show that the Lost Tribes are concealed somewhere outside of the nations of the earth.

1201

"Lo the people shall dwell alone, and shall not be reckoned among nations."

"And the captivity of the hosts of the children of Israel shall possess that of the Canaanites, even unto Zarephath (France), and the captivity of Jerusalem, which is in Sepharad (Spain), shall possess the cities of the south." See Obed. 20.

"This prophecy can only be explained by the present captivity, for in the Babylonish captivity the children of Israel were neither in France nor Spain."

"For the vision is yet for an appointed time, but at the end it shall speak, and not lie, though it tarry; wait because it will surely come, it will not tarry." Also Hab. 2:3.

"If they have merit by good works, I will hasten it; it shall come before the appointed time; but if they have no merit it shall come in its appointed time, which is stipulated and fixed, and which is known to the Divinity only. Thus saith the Lord, Keep ye judgment and do justice; for My salvation is near to come, and My righteousness to be revealed."

"The learned Rabbi Simon says the existence of the world depends on three things, viz.: Justice, Truth, and Peace."

"The flowers appear on the earth, the time of the singing birds is come, and the voice of the turtle is heard in our land." Sol. Song, 2:12.

"There is nothing better for a man than that he should eat and drink, and that he should make his soul enjoy good in his labor. This is so. I saw that it was from God. And that every man should eat and drink, and enjoy the good of all his labor, it is the gift of God." Eccl. 2:24; also 3:13.

"There are twenty-four Hebrew authors who mention the River Sambatyon and the Ten Tribes."

"There are also sixty authors who have written about the Ten Tribes.

"Two and a half are in Europe, Africa, Italy, Turkey, Holland, France, Germany and Poland, etc.

"Sambatyon is beyond the mountains of Gozan. The two and a half are the tribes of Judah, the second tribe of

Benjamin, and the half of Manasseh. The high-priests and some of the Levites remained at Jerusalem, and they have kept their genealogies. The tribe of Levi has been preserved more distinct than any other tribes."

We see in Hebrew literature great attention has been given to keep track of the Lost Tribes. By consulting the following list, it will be seen that the Lost Tribes are scattered as widely as the race of man, and while all believe in the verity of the Lost Tribes, their residence is so confusing, that one is bewildered and lost, as badly as the Israelites themselves. While Hebrew writers are thus puzzled and cannot agree, we find Gentile writers who claim the Anglo-Saxons, the English-speaking race, to be the Lost Tribes and some even claim Queen Victoria to be a descendant of Jeremiah the prophet.

If we are to believe all these writers, they are not lost, but are a portion of almost all people of the earth. But without further speculation Hebrew authors locate them as follows:

In Gozan, Hobas, India, Kallikut, where there are fifteen hundred isles, peopled with Jews; in Portugal, Babylon, Huleaa, Armenia, Tripoli, Naples, Mesopotamia, Rehabat, where there are 7,000; in Carchemas, where there are 14,000; in Phombadita, where there are 900; in Obkera, where there are 25,000; in Resen, where there are 7,000; in Milus, where there are 15,000. In Alexandria, Assyria, Ethiopia, Abyssinia, Chaldea, Tartary, Poland, Muscovy, Sumatra, Ceylon, East Indies, China, Georgia, around the Caspian Sea, Hyrcanea, Lydia, Phrygia, Arabia, Carthagina, Damascus, Ispahan, Cush, Elam, the Isles of the West, which is America.

It is evident that while there is a general belief cherished by Jew and Gentile, that the Lost Tribes are a verity, is there anywhere evidence of a prophetic, scientific, scriptural, or the evidence of travelers and explorers, as strong and conclusive as given in this work?

From the first to the last chapter, I have aimed to present the matter as it appears to me.

A.W. Greely's Three Years in the Arctic:

1203

## THE HIDDEN WORLD

"As seen by me, however, it was a most extraordinary display of the curtain formation which covered the entire heavens, and was constantly changing, never quiescent even a second. The very magnificence of the display forbids any attempt at description. A very marked magnetic disturbance appeared at the same time and I ordered five-minute readings to take place until further orders. The range of the needle was considerably over 19 degrees 0'. At 8:35 A.M. Gottingen mean time, the magnetic variation was but 92 degrees 0' 51", 6 degrees West."

C.W. Henry, p. 412:

"A magnetic storm evidently raging, as the needle is on the jump all the time. A bright streamer sprang from the southern horizon, gradually approaching the zenith with a labored movement closely resembling the spasmodic puffings of smoke rising from a working locomotive. Another streamer darted with great rapidity from the northern sky, and passing through the zenith, reached the southern horizon, where it remained several minutes glowing with an intense brilliancy, which perceptibly enhanced the feeble light furnished by the rapidly departing sun."

This man seemed to be in the midst of the aurora borealis, as it flamed up north and south of him, and met at the zenith.

Henry says:

"The display was sufficient to attract for most of us, to hold us spellbound for more than twenty minutes, in a temperature of 66 degrees below freezing point.

"The aurora defies description; it is indescribable by words, and not to be pictured by painter's skill.

"Nothing can convey a conception of the richness and vividness of its colors and infinite variety of tints. Streams of every shade of green, from the softest apple or pea to the dark invisible green of the hemlock pine, harmoniously blend with the lovely tints of lilac and purple, with celestial blue of the canopy, and shining here for an instant and then playfully skipping to another part of the sky.

"The whole display, now and then united in a luminous half transparent curtain, from horizon to zenith, curling

1204

# THE HIDDEN WORLD

SKY, ELECTRIC SUN AND OCEAN IN INNER WORLD.

A, Sky.   B, Electric Sun.   C, Ocean.   D, Falls.

and expanding, rising and falling like waves of an angry ocean, and suddenly steadying down again, the predominating characteristic formations of the loose folds of a curtain, and veiling for a time the stars. Objects in the landscape were plainly visible. The height which the display maintained above the earth was at no time of a greater elevation than that of cumulus clouds."

G.W. Rice, p. 414:

"The colors were remarkably brilliant and varied. At the base, pink and violet, rapidly changing and interchanging. In the center, the colors were lighter, pale yellow, or straw color, or white. The light or illumina, was quite of the full moon, and not more than 100 feet from the earth."

W.S. Jewell says, page 415:

"Israel went to the magnetic observatory and found the magnetic needle very much disturbed in consequence, the entire heavens covered with all kinds of formations and the movements in changes of formations so rapid, that the eye could not follow them. The sky was entirely free from clouds, and the light of second magnitude, the stars eclipsed."

416. H.S. Gordins:

"The whole heavens seemed one mass of colored flames, arranged and disarranged and rearranged every instant. The display was so near the earth, that we repeatedly put up our hands as though we could touch something in doing so."

One of the most pathetic and heroic of human achievements along the Verge is the report of The Cruise of The Revenue Marine Steamer Corwin, by Capt. M.A. Healy, as recorded in Lieut. Greely's Three Years in the Arctic. We give a few quotations, and the discriminating reader will find in this report matters for and against the position taken in this book, and as I am seeking after the truth, I give them for whatsoever they may prove.

Greely's Book, July 1, 1884. - "A heavy gale broke up the ice, and drove it to the northward. Little could be done, a dense fog rendered unceasing vigilance imperative."

P. 24. - "If the ship is shut in, and she escapes being crushed, she will go northward in the drifting pack, from

1206

# THE HIDDEN WORLD

one to two knots per hour, and it will become necessary to abandon her."

P. 7, Nov. 3. - "The sky at noon, quite clear to the south, was very bright at the horizon. Ice was in motion, being moved by the tides up and down Kennedy's Channel, which was evidently open. Rain-water clouds were seen for some distance; but to the south there was an ice blink."

P. 8, Nov. 14. - "A wonderful magnetic storm. The auroral displays were magnificent on those days. The storm culminated on the 17th, on which date the magnetic needle ranged in variation over 19 degrees, and a brilliant aurora was visible continuously for 9 hours."

January 25. - "A temperature 50 degrees, (45-6,0), the lowest of the winter today."

P. 14, Feb. 25. - "The sun would have risen astronomically today, or at least the upper limb of it, but it did not."

P. 15, March 1. - "The first day of Spring found us with health and spirits unimpaired."

P. 19, April 2. - "It is likely there is open water in the polar sea. Open water and the disintegration of the polar pack near Black Horn Cliffs compelled Lieut. Lockwood to turn back."

P. 21. - "Thick water clouds were visible to north April 12. Misty clouds obscured the entire north horizon." He was at this time at 85 degrees north latitude. And what is singular, these clouds proved it to be warmer to the north, while according to all laws it should have been warmer at the south. Lieut. Greely records as his belief that at "the North and South Poles are glacial lands, entirely covered with ice-caps of enormous thickness; its shores or edges of its glaciers are washed by a sea, which from its size and high temperature, its ceaseless tides and strong currents, can never be entirely ice-clad."

He concedes that Nordenskjold, Nares, Commander Markham, Parry, Lockwood, the drifting of the Tegitthoff and Jeanetta, winter as well as summer, is confirmation strong of evidence of "an open polar sea," but he is not willing to admit "a navigable open polar sea."

1207

## THE HIDDEN WORLD

P. 26. - "The first flowers came June 14, only three days late, and the geese and ducks followed the next day."

P. 29. - "Lieut. Lockwood and Sergt. Brainard climbed the precipitous cliffs, attaining a altitude of 4,444, on a summit which was named Mount Difficult. 81 degrees N., 70 degrees 41' W."

P. 32. - "I could rarely see very far directly south, even from mountains, in consequence of the high ice-clad surface."

P. 246, Feb. 12. - "The roaring ice, a dismal, fateful sound to us, was heard nearly all day, and dense water clouds seen to the north and east."

P. 251, Feb. 19. - "Smith's Sound was an open sea, no ice of any kind was visible on its surface, and the waves and whitecaps were rolling in against the edge of the fast ice with a dismal roar, which sounded in our ears as a knell of our impending doom."

P. 252, Feb. 21. - "The sun has not yet been seen by any of us, but its rays have appeared to the northward, gilding the mountains near Cape Frazer."

P. 254. - "Water towards the north was visible as far as the eye could reach."

P. 260, March 11. - "The sun for the first time touched the roof of our wretched hut."

Now with due deference to Lieut. Greely's opinions, he gives facts which, rightly considered, weigh in favor of an open polar sea, and an open navigable one. The sun for the first time touched their hut. Then nothing but the sun could melt the ice, but north of him was an open sea of water as far as he could see; but all was ice and frost south of him, where the sun should have thawed south of him first. In the winter, the only open water was always north, rain clouds were always seen in the north in winter; these clouds belong only to a high temperature above the freezing point. South of him were vast fields of ice and frost, with no rain clouds, north was an open sea, rain clouds, ships and ice-fields, floating northward winter and summer. Mr. Greely speaks of a "high temperature" at the North Pole, of ceaseless tides and currents. Now only one thing could

1208

## THE HIDDEN WORLD

produce high temperature - heat. Where did that heat come from to make rain clouds and open seas north, and why should ships and ice float north winter and summer, while all was sealed with ice south of him? He mentions not seeing far to the south while on the mountains, and attributes it to high ice, but if the North Pole was ice-clad and as cold as he supposes, the higher ice should be north instead of south. Granting my theory to be true, Mr. Greely was on the descending part of the verge, and he was looking up when gazing south, and that foreshortened his vision. And when he abandoned his steamer in the ice, she was floating north towards the opening in the earth, and he went south and southwest towards Greenland, while his ship went into the interior world, and when God lifts the veil then we will hear from the lost Marine Steamer Corwin, and so many lost vessels which have never been heard from in this mysterious sea.

The British ships Alert and Discovery have placed on record that the open polar sea of Kane and Hays is a myth, and they believe no person can approach nearer to the pole than 400 miles.

Letting that go for what it is worth, the American explorer, Hays, in a letter to the New York Herald, reiterates his belief of an open polar sea, and he says as follows:

"Believing in an open polar sea, I think it can be navigated. The English expedition saw great quantities of ice. They never left the land, and along the land you always find ice in all Arctic waters. I believe I reached beyond the land belt of ice in 1861. With a boat I could have gone to the pole. An ice belt in summer depends much upon the prevailing wind, but as for any large body of water being at any time frozen over, even with the lowest temperature, it is unknown. Hudson's Bay, Baffin's Bay, and other Arctic waters, even though comparatively small, are never frozen over. The deep sea waters in all oceans and seas of the earth have a uniform temperature of about 35 degrees. The surface water under the equator is often 85 degrees. In the Arctics it is generally down to 29 degrees. I have seen

1209

waves rolling at 50 degrees below zero, without a particle of ice. The next day, when the air fell to a calm, the whole sea was covered with a crystal mantle. The Arctic Ocean is over 2000 miles in diameter, and if anybody will once get over the land-clinging ice belt, and into the middle of the Arctic Sea, he might sail all about there to his heart's content, and I, for one, cannot see why this English expedition should so soon have abandoned the field. There are certain avenues to this great, mysterious, unknown water.

"There is the oft-tried Behring Strait. There is Baffin's Bay. There is the Spitzbergen Sea and the Greenland Sea. In this last quarter the Germans have found A NEW LAND. This land lies midway between Spitzbergen and Nova Zembla, which land I predicted many years ago in an address before the American Geographical Society."

In view of the near approach of the coming of Christ and the hiding of the Tribes in the North, as shown by the Scriptures, and their return to Jerusalem, the subject is one of absorbing interest to the Christian. In considering the question, I feel that I have not lowered the standard of morality or written aught that will shake the faith of any devout Christian, or trench upon the boundaries of eternal truth. Nor have I written anything that I would blush to confront on the day of general account.

And, finally, in closing and bidding the reader farewell, "Let us hear the conclusion of the whole matter, fear God, and keep His commandments."

"For God shall bring every work into judgment, with every secret thing, whether it be good or whether it be evil." (Eccl. 12: 13, 14.)

No one can doubt but what there is something at the Verge strange and not yet comprehended.

Why does the magnetic needle always point towards the North?

Why at the Verge does it "always swing to and fro in an uneasy way?"* (*Vol. I. of Lieutenant Greely's Three Years of Arctic Service, p. 128.)

Why should the needle point to the North over all other

# THE HIDDEN WORLD

parts of the earth?

Why not point towards the equator, the largest part of the globe?

Why not point towards the South Pole? and why not "swing to and fro in a restless, uneasy way over the Southern Verge" as it does over the Northern?

For some unexplained reason the needle South of the Verge always points North, and on the Northern Verge "swings to and fro in an uneasy way."

Until science explains, all must admit there is something mysterious there!

So deeply has this impressed the world, that eleven nations have established stations in the far North "for developing meteorology and in extending our knowledge of terrestrial magnetism."* (*Vol. I. of Lieutenant Greely's Three Years of Arctic Service, p. 21.)

These nations are the United States, Austria, Hungary, Denmark, Finland, France, Germany, Great Britain and Canada, Holland, Norway, Russia, and Sweden.* (*Ibid., p. 23.)

On page 58 Greely says: "During the day and evening the compass unfortunately gave us much trouble, being very unreliable." And on page 128 he states: "In the magnetometer, a small magnet, freely suspended by a single fiber of untwisted silk, swings readily in an horizontal direction. This magnet at Conger was never quiet, not even on what are technically known as calm days, but swung to and fro in a restless, uneasy way, which at various times impressed me with an uncanny feeling quite foreign to my nature. As it swung to right and left, its movement was clearly outlined on a fixed illuminated glass scale, which served as a background, and the extreme oscillations, seen through a small telescope by the observer, were recorded. A magnetic needle, nicely and delicately balanced in the middle latitudes, assumes a nearly level position. At Conger, however, the needle, adjusted so that it can move freely in a vertical plane, shows a strong tendency to assume an upright position." Lieutenant Greely shows the variation to be more than one-fourth the circuit of the globe.

1211

## THE HIDDEN WORLD

On the Verge, therefore, is the point where the "magnetic needle swings to and fro and up and down." That furnishes scientific evidence of the mystery hanging around that part of the globe. Over every other part of the world man can tell his whereabouts by the needle, which is said to point unerringly towards the North Pole. But on the Verge it swings "to and fro." Here man meets in the magnetic needle another obstacle, which God has erected as one of the bewildering barriers to shield the children of Israel, and shut them out "from being counted among the nations."

Strangest and strongest is the attraction of the needle northward and its bewildering variation on the Verge. He adds to the Arctic cold, the frozen sea, six months of darkness, the strange antics of the magnetic needle!

It goes a long way to prove there is no North Pole such as Newton teaches and geography maps out. But along the Verge man must stop and pay tribute to a paramount law. Here is the limit of his dominion.

The needle pointing downwards and upwards shows an outer and inner crust to the earth; an outer and an inner world, where the magnet balances; an equilibrium of forces. The swinging of the needle "to and fro," east and west, shows along the Verge to be the true North Pole; that the ideal geographical North Pole is a myth of science, and that the Verge is the only North Pole.

Am I not, therefore, justified in claiming that, if there is a mystery along the Verge, that there is more Beyond the Verge?

Here is the one spot where man is lost. He has crossed the world east and west in his circum-polar voyages; he has sailed round and round the Verge for centuries, but across this terra incognita no human footstep but the lost of Israel are permitted to tread.

Man may stand on the Verge, but can never travel into the inner world until the "fulness of time." He may stand confounded, looking at the "restless, uneasy swinging of the needle;" looking, like Lieutenant Greely, until he, too, feels "an uncanny feeling" creep over him.

He may stand on the Verge and behold the solid globe as

1212

he has been taught to regard it, held with adamantine grasp, forever pointing its north end where its magnetic needle whirls towards the North Star - a star fixed at one spot in the heavens, so far as the earth is concerned, while all the other stars, constellations, asteroids, pliades, comets, and suns are wheeling, turning, spinning, and speeding towards a common center called Hercules.

But the world is never permitted to deviate. Its northern end is held in everlasting position towards the north star, where all attraction is and all Scripture points; and I trust that, if not convinced of the verity of this book, that you will have your faith in the power of God strengthened, and will admit that there is something unknown and mysterious BEYOND THE VERGE.

# THE HIDDEN WORLD
# Formula From

1214

## THE HIDDEN WORLD
# the Underworld

**Harte Manville lowered himself into a cavern; and found a mad world.**

1215

## THE HIDDEN WORLD
# By RICHARD S. SHAVER

I AM AN explorer, by name Harte Manville. My face is badly scarred, one eye is missing. My hair is grizzled, but I am still strong and active.

Ten long years ago I had first heard that some works by the storied races of the Gods still existed, deep in earth. While reading a tale by Brandoch Daha called "The Womb of Tanit" I had realized that mysterious and perhaps immortal life might still exist in the bowels of old Mother Earth. I understood from his words that some of my experiences which I had explained to myself as hallucinations induced by privation had been actual occurrences of immense significance. I mused that it was an infinite shame such sincere and top-rank research minds of earth had to disguise their work as fiction to get it before the general mind at all.

Overcome with curiosity as to Daha's reactions to my own experiences, I was curious too as to what he might have to tell a man who knew some of the truths of the underworld. How he might loosen up and talk when he met a man who knew which small parts of his stories were fiction and which great parts were not. I sought him out and called upon him. I was not wrong. Mr. Daha was very glad to see me.

During the course of our night-long conversation our discussion touched on the subjects of the secret surviving worship of the ancient Moon Goddess, Tanit, and details of my expedition to plumb the depths of the bottomless hole in the Cave of the Bats in Virginia. The fact that we both knew that immortal beings have existed, do now exist, and will continue to exist, brought up naturally enough the age-old question:

"What is the Secret which keeps such life from dying as other life does?"

I remember his words:

"There have been many things mistaken for the Secret of Life. The phrase should mean 'continue existence without aging'. All right, this time it does. But you will have to grasp with your head firmly, not sleepily, to see the big meaning that can lie in simple phrases.

"Since before the flood, there exist in legends stories of those creatures, the Gods, who were immortal. Also tales of those other kind, of scholars who learned the secrets of immortality; tales of magi, of genis; of peris, of fairies, of immortal witch-maids, of sorcerers, of enchanters. An enormous amount of smoke comes out of antiquity about 'the secret of life' which in modern words means 'how to exclude the poisons that cause age from the human body.' All that antique smoke indicates very strongly that once that true fire of wisdom from Prometheus existed; that storied Atlantis, full of immortals, was; that the Gods did tread earth, sinking ankle deep in solid rock.

"Let us go over that possibility between us. First, we will look at the beginning of life. Why is it young, and not old, like its mother? The womb of the mother holds the flesh of the baby, it is young, she is often aged. Why is this flesh not also old? Because, interposed between her body and the embryo are the walls of the womb. Everything that goes into the baby must pass through the food tube which passes through a large filtering organ called the placenta. Obviously some poison is removed. The baby's flesh is growing at a swift rate, the flesh of the aging mother is shrinking; it is more disintegrant than integrant."

HE PAUSED. We both had a drink, he lit a cigar; but before I could get going he started on.

"I once translated an ancient German work by Bokbe. It was a translation by him of a very old Arabian work, which was in turn from the Egyptian. God knows how old the original is. I will read you my translation."

He got up, pulled a pile of manuscripts from a drawer, and selecting one, began:

"After Atlantis sank beneath the blue roll of ocean sea, there still existed scattered about earth similar cities to Atlantis. These cities were not surface cities but were buried beneath the earth in great and deep caves to protect them from the deadly sun which they knew to be the cause of age! But now the cities were empty and dead of any intelligent life; their mighty corridors echoed to no laughing feet of the young immortal they had once bred into the storied races of the Gods. Instead, there slunk about their streets the pariahs, the lepers, the outcasts and criminals of the upper world, fled from the too frequent anger of the ignorant men of the surface. They had found a refuge in these secret lost cities.

"Now, the long vanished residents of these caverns had once been numerous and wealthy in the products that immortal minds which had conquered the problem of death could give. The God race, long ago had 'ascended into the blue of heaven in their fiery chariots,' the nomads told each other in the torch-lit darkness, as they gazed wonderingly about them at the machinery whose uses even the wisest man has not yet guessed and whose uses the ignorant tomb robbers and pariahs dismissed with the single word - magic. But that first wondering ignorance of the near-wild discoverers of the dwelling places of the Atlanteans' neighbors did not continue. For one day the inevitable happened.

"In a luxurious living place where the pillars were of sculptured metal set with sparkling brilliants like fruit and covered with the glitter of green glass-like leaves as a tree, and the walls alive with fearfully writhing figures in a frozen dance, a lonesome, lost child touched a button in a wall projection and screamed as the figures came to life and moved magically upon the wall. But there was love in the meaning of their movements, and there was thought in the walls. The thought that the waves from the wall carried to the child was a force that commanded him to love and to learn, to study and to think, to watch and to want, to become aware of what life could be and to strive mightily and cannily toward the things he wanted most. The force commanded him in such a way that he became the servant of the force.

"For in the wall was a strange thing that the Gods left, a machine that entertained and taught people and many and long were the hours the child spent in that chamber before stealing back to his mother. When he left he did not know enough to touch the button again and the machine ran on. Thus began the life of the First of the Latter Gods. Over his head stormed the armies of our first Pharoah, but the child heard them not; he was deep underground watching the magic of pictures that moved and talked, and listening with his brain to thought from a wire in the machine.

"HE BROUGHT his playmates into the secret of the magic button that made the figures on the wall move and live and that made the big room fill with heady music and with mighty waves of commanding thought. So it was that magic became the secret of outcasts, and the latter Gods the people who guarded the secret of the caverns from the scorned and feared men of the surface. Many and awesome were those secrets and poor and few their uses for them, but still magic lived again on earth. For they went to the surface with their strange secret weapons, fooling the surface folk and taking their gold and food and returning again to the depths, laughing with their talk of the sport it had been to make them think that ghosts were abroad, that demons and efrits had come for their souls or their gold.

"But some, like the boy who switched on the teaching machine, became aware of the great beauty and the mighty learning that lay in those machines, waiting only for the touch of curious fingers on the right button to spring into active life. These children of the caves became habitual explorers of the vast mysterious recesses, stretching on in ever different wonders into the depths, into the very heart of earth.

"Some of the machines gave off a sweet, overpowering pleasant beneficial force, invisible except as irridescence, yet force that awakened their minds and bodies into furious life and growth. Since the ancients were master builders these mechanisms did not wear out easily, having been built to endure. These inquiring, exploring young people, by virtue of the growth force that was in the magic machines, became mighty beings of vastly superior abilities and strengths. Beings superior to ordinary men by so far that they were, in truth, Gods!

"These gathered men about them, taught them the use of the stored weapons, the aircraft that lay in the ancient underground airship houses, and began again to build as the ancient Gods had builded. Great sections of earth came under their secret rule. In the northland the immortals ruled as Odin and as Wotan. In Greece as Zeus and his followers. In the sea as Oceanus, Jehovah, Jupiter. There were many who learned in time which machines had the power to make them nearly immortal and who in time came to rule their part of the world. Some of them built surface cities. In the northland the fame of Asgard and Valhalla reached far, though a man came to fear to talk to his God lightly. But the little people are great gossips.

"Then a strange Evil came upon these hidden rulers of earth; the Evil that culminated in Ragnorak and Armageddon and in eventual Hell and Earth's near domination by Hell. The Twilight and Death of the Latter Gods was not a pleasant time. For the sun is a fearful and deadly thing in the same way that glow-metal is fearful and deadly, and though these Latter Gods learned much, they did not learn that the sun throws an invisible pollen of poison that infects all the energy of earth with a horrible accumulating ever-fire that is the true cause of age. The machines that gave them their strength and life and growth contained filters that swept the energy flows clean of these sun poisons; but this second race of Gods did not learn the secret of the filters and well though they were builded the machines at last became saturated with the deadly rust.

"NOW, A good man is one whose will is a flow of beneficial energy generated by healthy cells, and his will is a force bringing only good to all things. But as the machines became filled with the disintegrant motes from the sun's infection of earth energy, these machines in turn affected the great bodies and minds of the Latter Gods with a destructive flow of energy. A destructive, evil will, gradually took the place of good will in their mighty frames. So it was that one by one the underground cities became Hells where men were brought to amuse the mad minds of their masters with unending agonies, for a man can suffer long when his life is renewed from the old machines. Many of the machines

## THE HIDDEN WORLD

still gave off a force that kept life in the body even though that body were racked with tortures that else would cause death a thousand times.

"Gradually this evil stole over earth and, not knowing the cause - the failure of the filters in the machines to remove the disintegrant dust of the sun - they fought each other in such battles as still live in the mouths of men.

"Evil and good fought titanically for possession of earth, and Evil won, for the ancient polluted mechanisms turned even the best willed men into Demons of destructive will. Magic lived on as evil witchery, as 'the works of the devil' and the secret people of the underworld were feared and hated as the curse they were. They came to the surface in fierce raids and returned again before the still sane remnants of those who knew of the caves could catch them.

"Here and there the white magic lived on, ever hunted by the maddened men of the underworld who were no longer men but devils who strove to destroy all wisdom so that no one should ever be able to resist them. How well they succeeded is shown by the darkness of centuries -"

Daha's almost chanting voice ceased. He returned the paper to the drawer. Then his voice went on, almost as if to himself.

"Those are an ancient God's words!

"Sometimes during the near past," he continued, "probably soon after the advent of gunpowder, it is said that they practised blowing up the entrances to the underworld, to trap each other and to keep themselves safe from their eternal raids on each other; that now all trace of these passages is lost. Others say that it is not true, and that one reason Earth men are so backward is that still, even today, wild men come up from deep in the earth; wild men with the weapons and the tools of Gods, and steal secretly about the world killing men of science so quietly and in such a way that other men never suspect the true cause of death. These hint that the death of such men as Pierre Curie are not accidents, that Pierre was murdered because that is the hereditary custom of these things from the depths - to kill those who approach in their studies the use of rays, the properties of magnets, and strange virtues that lie in synthetic animal magnetism. Some hint that the Legend of the Wandering Jew, of the Watcher, of the Hag, of the Howling Mother of Sin herself, of witches and goblins, are still living beings who live for no one knows how many centuries, yet who become evil in time even today because they never learn that the antique generators always degenerate into generators of an evil force that overwhelms and distorts the will into a kind of hypnosis of destructive command. That men can never recover from these beings, for they have the weapons of the Gods, as well as certain wisdoms long handed down secretly. That this evil hypnosis by the defective machinery that they now build or find still can never be fought against, for men are too foolish - the wild devil-things of the caverns too wily and well equipped.

"Then, too, there are very definite tales that have come upon them. These are served by the better of the smaller beings of the caverns and sometimes men from the surface too. But men are supposed not to live down there long except they are lucky and very strong. The conditions are too different.

"CERTAIN it is that many men secretly believe this is the real cause of all man's troubles and wars. That these beings from the darkness come up still, flying great globes of metal in which is machinery that controls men's minds and actions so that it is but as playing marbles or chess for them to choose sides; and each side backing armies of the surface people play with them as the little Dutchmen of Rip van Winkle played at nine-pins: play with armies of nations at a game they call Bickro - in their tongue - meaning bickering robots. That what is to us a war is to them but a game.

"All this and much else of a still wilder kind is whispered of and believed by many men just as magic and witches were whispered of and believed in Medieval times, though not aloud, for men would then and now tap their heads and scoff did anyone say aught of the truth of the underworld."

We talked of many things which I cannot mention, but one

1222

thing I learned well and that was where to look for the secret of immortal life. For I had entered and explored a bit of those endless caverns that honeycomb the depths of earth, but I had not realized that in the records of those people who built them lay the formulae and processes which had made them immortal. I knew that much writing still lined the walls of those tremendously antique dwellings. I knew that sealed-in portions containing libraries of books whose pages were of indestructible metal still lay untouched, but that anyone had ever translated any of the language or thought of doing so had never entered my head. And to tell anyone of the existence of actual working machines and written books built in a time so antique it is forgotten was, I knew, impossible.

But Brandoch Daha knew, had even obtained from a miner one volume of the metal books and had worked out a key which opened that mighty thought to the man who dared to enter the caverns. But he was too old; and, too, he knew of the dread and incomprehensible creatures who dwell in those caves. His word pictures of these beings had not made the project revolving in mind any more inviting. But try it I would, I knew that, for I knew myself. No one felt and answered the lure of magic more readily than myself and those books were the source from which came the 'Magic Books' which in all legends and tales of the past are the strength and wisdom of the sorcerers.

"Now that I knew the origin of these ancient tombs from which rose the mightiest power spoken of in all the past of man, now that I knew it was true wisdom in those books and that they could be gotten at if one were hardy and intrepid enough, the Devil himself - and well it might be one as great lying in wait in the darkness of those endless giants' warrens - could not keep me from trying to get them.

"So it was that my long trek started."

\* \* \*

LOWERED down the shaft of the Bottomless Pit, a good mile of cable unreeling above me, I searched the walls eagerly for an opening. At last it came, one of those perfectly round, apparently metal line holes which are the only entrance into the caves that were homes of the Gods. What they were originally intended for I don't know. Perhaps all that is left of a breather pipe to the surface and the pipe, of less durable materials, disappeared to leave an opening in the inaccessible caves of the past. Inaccessable because the walls were made so hard no metal will cut them.

A few sways of my body and my cable became a pendulum to place me on a shelf a few feet from that opening. Now, again, I must enter the dwelling place of Evil, the home of Dread; the beautiful structures, once the homes of God-like beings, now the dens of incomprehensible, often giant things whose endless struggles for existence made these caves a Hell. This search must not fail, nothing must stop me, for now that I had the key to their language – any bit of their immense lore of science which I might bring back could and most probably would change the whole future life of man. And they knew the cause of age and had conquered it! I must not fail!

Load after load of equipment and food came down the cable, and the telephone line which connected this remote hole in the depths with the surface world, which would await my call for return did months or years lapse before I used it. I set up the radio wave emitting apparatus which would activiate a needle in a radio compass at my belt every ten minutes so that I would never lose the direction of my base and my exit. Finally, with many of the sensations that Theseus must have had as he searched for the Minotaur, I set off through the vaulted halls lined with majestic and mighty mechanisms, covered with the dust of endless centuries. This dust was my insurance of safety for when I neared THEM, the dust would contain footprints and paths.

I came to vast machines built for unknowable uses as big as a city block. Often they were topped by a seat, massive and huge for a giant's form. I had seen some of these before, but had not thought there was much use in looking them over carefully as their age must have rendered them useless. It was whispered that some of these ancient mechanisms still worked.

I mounted the six-foot steps leading up to the great seat of a machine. An infinitely bewildering array of switches, buttons and levers were banked across the panel in front of the seat. Ten feet up, where a twenty-foot giant's eyes would be, was a shimmering white expanse. Was it a screen? Tentatively I pulled a few levers. A soft, thrilling humming throbbed through the vastness of the mechanism beneath me. On the white expanse a picture appeared, a scene on the surface of earth. I turned a huge knob and the scene changed. Like Odin's eye it swept across the country, how far, how many endless miles that penetrating view ray swept its automatic focus, I could not say.

Now, in ancient tales, such stories as those of Solomon's ring, of Merlin, of Aladdin's lamp, said that magic machinery was capable of nearly any miracles asked of it. Of what else was this monstrous machine capable? I soon found out.

I WAS looking at a surface scene, a farm house in front of which was a big elm and leaning backward to see better in the screen above my head my hand inadvertently grasped a lever to support me. There in the scene of the house and elm a great wind sprang up whirling and whirling around the house. As I pondered whether the wind appearing so suddenly was a part of nature or made by the machine my other hand rested on a lever at the side of the huge seat and instantly an awful bolt of force struck the elm in the center of the screen and it disappeared, leaving nothing but a hole in the earth and a cloud of dust whirling in the wind. This machine was quite a plaything, I decided. I had better learn something about it. This eye, which like Odin's, seemed able to go everywhere and see everything, was just the thing with which to explore these caverns with and save my feet.

These caverns are not as one would picture them, full of stalagmites and stalactites and dripping with moisture. Quite the contrary, they are dry. The walls are of hardened, impenetrable rock and every half-mile great metal doors seal the passages from all water and air. Thick dust is the only sign of the passage of time; and this varies: some places there is very little, for the doors keep the caves sealed tightly. Some are corroded, though, and here is much dust and some dampness.

I swept the ray up the miles of caves beyond me, drinking in the colorful beauty of the ancient dwellings - the story of tremendous life that every bit of the work tells.

There is a brooding, deserted-temple atmosphere about these ancient homes. The mighty presence of the past life left something that still lives, quiescent but awesome: the vast machines, beautiful as no other machinery on earth, the silence, the waiting power. The ray swept along the far-reaching avenues. What was I looking for? Well, I found something, I can tell you.

They sprang into the vision screen suddenly as the ray swept past; they were gone. It took me an hour to find them again. Living things! Down here! I had heard of them, seen some strange things before. But I had not had an Odin's eye to watch them.

They were in what had once been some huge ancient's living quarters. The bed was a tremendous affair some twenty by thirty feet. Sprawled about its expanse were a dozen creatures asleep in the rays that bathed the bed. The creatures were human, apparently, yet not human at all, on second examination. Living in the depths had changed them; they were as different from men as a potato sprout in the cellar is from a potato plant in the field.

The ray brought to the screen not only the things to be seen, but an augmentation of the things to be heard. I distinctly heard the creatures thinking, as well as saw them.

Their thought was as alarming as their appearance. The rays that bathed the ancients' bed were pleasure rays as well as soporific rays. They induced an ultra-pleasant dream state in which the will of the sleeper found every wish coming true, tremendously true. But these creatures were not men; they were - degenerates - things.

1226

Their wishes and dreams were of blood and death and tortures for their enemies and little else, for all the creatures they dreamed of seemed enemies. I had an impulse - a strong one - to pull that lever that had blotted out the elm tree and turn these sleeping curses into drifting dust. They called themselves Hobloks. A meanness sat on their faces, looking out and hating all life.

IN APPEARANCE the sleepers were like fearfully anaemic jitterbugs, small, with pipestem arms and legs, pot bellies, huge protruding eyes and wide, idiotically grinning mouths. Super-goofy, I believe modern youth would call them. They wore clothes as men do, apparently clothes recently from the surface world, and as I tinkered with the focus of the monster eye in front of me a modern truck spring into view, a trailer job closed and fitted inside for living. There must be a way of driving down here from the surface. These Things had contact with the surface! I must know more about that.

In another chamber near the sleepers were a group of normal-appearing people apparently fresh from the surface. Reading their thought I gathered that they had answered an ad in the paper; had been hired only to find at the end of their journey this place, and themselves in the hands of the Hobloks. They had been locked in for days and were completely at sea mentally. Just what did the Hobloks want with them? Could I get the answer by looking at the sleepers' thoughts?

One of them was dreaming of the reward he would receive for turning over the captives at their destination. And what a destination! If it was anything like the Things' mental pictures, it was some place. Much deeper in earth, it was; once the home of some tremendous being. The chambers were many city blocks in width and fantastically sculptured, lined with machanisms. A fierce activity filled the place.

Sometime in the past, I gathered, some one of these cavern dwellers had turned on a growth force generator and lain down to sleep in it. The results were that he had

1227

become another greater life. He had not turned it off, but stayed beside it and growth had made a super being of him. It was not balanced growth. He was a vast mass of pink flesh with sprouts of peculiar life protruding from him. This Thing was the boss of the place. The captives were destined to serve this mass of flesh. His appetite for women was enormous, to judge by the harem that surrounded him, stroking the quivering pinkness, carefully removing the sprouts when they were ripe, dancing for the vast eyes that surmounted the awful pile of flesh. I did not like this modern god.

In other chambers men were working on the ancient mechanisms, taking them apart, studying them, putting them back together. I could not get from the creature's mind more than a glimmer of what really was going on except that he knew the people laboring there were under a strong compulsion. They were robots to others who made them work. The workers were technically trained men from the surface while the masters were cavern beings whom the workers never saw. That the masters were also under compulsion from the mountain of flesh seemed likewise true.

In front of the mountain of flesh a woman lay writhing in an agony of desire. Wires led to her from several mechanisms within reach of the monster's hands. He made adjustments now and then on the dials of the panels. He seemed to be breathing in the augmented vitality of the woman. His huge eyes ogled as he strove to bend toward her. As her anguished limbs and striving body thrashed to a crescendo of awful torment - her heart gave way, her body stilled; she died. The creature in whose dreaming mind I watched this scene was serenely, greatly satisfied at this death. So I gathered was the man mountain.

As I watched, her body was removed by red-masked attendants and replaced by another living beauty from the surface. The scene began again in the dreamer's mind; he enjoyed it greatly.

THIS god was mad. Somewhere in the depths his private hell was functioning. These captives were destined for
1228

his peculiar pleasures. Many of them were women. The others were technical engineers, the best minds an ad for trained men at a fantastically high salary had brought. How long had this been going on? The sleeping creature did not know; all his life so far as I knew.

But such things could not go on without men's knowledge, you say. Well, having used the ray machinisms and knowing their power and seeing such things, I say they can and do go on. For no one could approach a listening ray mech without its operator hearing. No person could think or do a thing other than the operator willed if he were watched and ruled by an Odin's ray. The caverns do exist. I was there.

It suddenly occurred to me that I might be in danger from these goofy Hobloks or from the will-less men who served the formless master in the Hoblok's dream. And once they located me, away would go all my dreams of ancient books and the formula for eternal life which the legends so repeatedly attribute to them. I could not fail! The whole future of man would depend on my search, were it successful, for any bit of their ancient science could change the whole course of earth science. If they spotted me on a ray I would have short shrift I knew from the dreams of killing that filled their sleeping minds.

I decided to attempt to see this private Hell with the giant ray at which I sat. It was the safest way to learn what it was all about. Certainly I could not proceed on my search without knowing where it lay and how to avoid falling into the growth monster's hands.

A couple of hours patient searching of the depths with the amazingly penetrative ray finally revealed on of the workrooms where the red-masked servants of the monster stood guard over the enslaved engineers. I quickly understood their slavery, for a strong generator of thought waves filled the room with a command, abstract but powerful; stronger than any thought they themselves could possibly generate.

"Work and construct from these ancient machines powerful pleasure machines for my enjoyment," were the thought waves.

1229

## THE HIDDEN WORLD

Thus these highly trained men from the surface, brought into the presence of this strong thought command, worked at the construction of pleasure nerve stimulators for the mountain of pink flesh. Worked till they dropped, only to get up and work again.

Reading the minds of the red-masked men who stood about like guards I found little but a habit of obedience to commands from their master. They had very little mental activity; had been practically robots since children.

So that huge Thing of flesh that had once been something like a man was perpetually bathed in hundreds of high-power stimulative pleasure rays. His was a tremendous energy devoted to ways of feeling ever greater sensuous pleasure; pleasure which, to him, consisted in stimulating a woman till life energy killed her by its intensity. Here in this underworld he had found ways of getting a steady supply of prisoners and an ever greater amount of pleasure stimulating force rays. I did not like this Thing whom his slaves called Mula. No, I did not like him.

SO AFTER more protracted fishing with the mighty mechanism I had activated, but was finding difficulty in learning to use accurately, I finally brought Mula himself into direct focus, saw him vast on the center of the screen, smelt the sweat from that soft, enormous, hundred tons of corrupt growth. I heard the thought that ran through the awful head of him. Listen carefully and I will try to tell you what a thing like that thinks.

"The growth which has come upon me depends entirely on certain kinds of rays which the ancients knew how to make. My robots are fast developing similar devices to the one which made me into this mighty life and then wore out to leave me to grow old, never to move toward pleasure in others' death. Ah, the sweet agonies of these creatures desiring love - love - and getting more desire of love till their fluttering little energies burst their flesh and fly away. Soon my slaves will bring the growth rays and I will start to grow again, to grow and feel young again, gloriously alive as I was centuries ago before the first ancient growth ray wore out. Then I will grow and eat and grow and fill all the caverns with myself; I will be all. By that time I will have learned to consume all matter, to make all things into myself. I will be Earth!"

"Hell," I thought to myself, "the darned Thing is senile, is a crazy old man; maybe once a super being, centuries ago; but now the strength in him has kept him alive while age has made a destructive idiot of him."

Just here my troubles began, for, hearing thought as I did it had never occurred to me that the one I listened to could also hear me. That there might be a way of handling this instrument so that I could hear without being heard had never occurred to me; nor had I realized that it might work both ways. Anyway, the ancient giant of growth heard me. I heard his commands ring on my ears as they leaped from his "robot-make" machine as he called it, a device making his thought so strong that the robots must obey it.

"Some surface man is spying on me with a ray," I heard him thinking. "Find him. Kill him or bring him to me at once!"

I heard him mentally rubbing his hands in anticipation of the cojing delight of slowly killing me after he learned if there were others to worry about.

A cold sweat broke out on my face. I had no wish to become part of Mula's pleasure.

My life right now depended on whether Mula's creatures had equipment that would reach this spot. There was little I could do about it.

All at once I thought of the lever which had destroyed the elm tree in my first experimental manipulations. I got Mula's bulk in the exact center of my screen and pulled that lever fully expecting to see Mula dissolve into drifting dust. Instead he let out the most unearthly howl of pain it has ever been my pleasure to hear. Too much rock, I realized, between us for the bolt to be fully effective. Well, it was something to hear Mula howl and see his endless ripples of flesh quivering in agony like a scared dowager's double chins endlessly repeated and endlessly twitching in pain and terror. I stood up on the huge seat and howled into the

1231

screen:

"Mula, if you don't instantly call off your animals I'll fill you so full of pain you'll wish you weren't quite so big."

**HE PROBABLY** didn't speak English but he grasped the thought behind the words.

Mula proved to be just a big, bad sissy after all. He couldn't take it. He was all placating, ingratiating thought as he gave orders sending his men back to their former positions. But I was stuck. I had to hold that ray on Mula and give him a dose of pain everytime the thought occurred to him that perhaps I wasn't listening and he could now arrange my demise. I decided I needed help. Riding herd on senile super man Mula was not a one-man job.

There was only one place I could get help - that was that truckload of fresh surface captives waiting in the chamber by the sleeping Hobloks. I would have to do the job in a hurry or the man-mountain would put one over on me.

I swung the huge eye to its former focus on the sleeping crew of underworld slavers and in a twinkling had obliterated the bed on which they lay in their poisonous dreams. I had no desire to play with them; they seemed to know their way around down here and Mula was plenty to handle just now. I blasted away the locked door to the chamber of the captives and standing up to the screen yelled at their bewildered faces:

"Get in that truck and start driving. I'll tell you how to get out of here."

For the next hour I was busy as a postman on Christmas Eve, swinging over to Mula and giving him a mocking tee-hee and a jolt of juice and swinging back to figure out the path the truck must take to reach me. But the hour stretched into days.

Mula was in one vast quiver of frustrated rage fearing to give orders to seek me out and yet unable to bear the loss of his power which had been undisputed for centuries, from what I had read in his mind. He was pretty sure I was one of the Hobloks who had acquired big ideas on the surface and had decided to turn the tables on his meaty Majesty. I

1232

did not feel greatly complimented, for those anaemic super-goofs were not my idea of what to be mistaken for. Nevertheless I mouthed the mean-sounding nothings I had seen them use in their dreams and certainly I took as much delight in tormenting Mula as I knew they would have taken in tormenting me. How I detested that pile of fat, inhuman appetite!

HOW had a growth force generator succeeded in creating this monstrous pollution? An increase in growth rate, in the supply of growth causing material, should result in an enhanced power of perception, a greater awareness of beauty, a mightier will to create, a really superior being with a will to make life something fine to have. How had a growth force mechaniam succeeded in creating this monstrous pollution? It was too much for me. Even if the machine had failed centuries before something of the fine qualities it must have helped to grow in man should have remained. Was age itself, then, such a cause of corruption? It appeared so. But as I watched the ancient life in him I learned what really made him the horror he was.

From several places which I could not locate, rays came into the hall where his bulk lay - rays which subtly caused him to think. As I listened to these rays which seemed unnoticed by Mula I heard an idiotic murmur of utterly degenerate thought. Some creature in the distance was at some machine watching Mula and the idiocy of the thought was, through the strength of the great augmentation, causing Mula to think in the same way. Though I could see this occur, Mula was apparently oblivious of these creatures; yet, they were making him think!

I finally got it through me just how this had made Mula the thing he was. These creatures were the wild natural inhabitants of the caverns who had lived there since earliest times, fishing in the underground rivers, stealing some food from surface fields. Those I had just killed as they slept were some whom Mula had impressed into his service, but all through the caverns were some of these thin little half-men with protruding eyes adapted to the dark. Their only play was turning on the old machine to see and talk to surface people and to each other in the depths. Always some of them had watched Mula, his growth and his behavior, and the latter was much a product of their own idiotic little brains augmented by the mighty machines until the constant pressure of the great rays on him had produced an hypnotic effect on Mula. He had become as they were by the long effect of the distant, unnoticed watching. They were clever imitators just as monkeys are and instinctively when one looked at them over the ray, they felt it and put on an unobtrusive mental attitude. It was evidently this habit which kept Mula from realizing what a great effect they had on him.

Watching them I also learned that they really hated and feared Mula and when he was unaware of them they had a way of introducing another destructive ray into the screen. Thus, with a strong magnification of Mula on their screen they would watch his brain and body with their small rays which the big machine augmented and carried into Mula's body. So it was, in truth, that he was nearly an idiot, as the connecting nerves of his brain had been mostly destroyed. He considered them as his allies and servants. It never seemed to occur to him that they were in truth his death.

This very subtle whittling at his huge brain, as habitual to them as a mouse's nibbling is to a mouse, was the very cause of Mula's oblivious attitude, as well as the hypnotic effect of all such huge rays. They did not want Mula to think of them and Mula obeyed the huge impulse post-hypnotically.

IT TOOK several hours of observation for all this to be understood by myself. The creatures were very interesting. They watched surface people continually, whispering complicated lies in their ears. This was one of their greatest pleasures; in fact they had almost no use for the truth. Their whole life was one of watching over the big rays and figuring out childish deviltries to inflict on the surface men. Their secret - where and what they were - the surface men never seemed to figure out. Though most of them suffered from them more or less, they never spoke to each other about it for fear of being considered mad. Believing in invisible imps! It was too fantastic and stupid a thing.

This thing I watched, I slowly realized, had been going on since the earliest times. It was a fixed, repetitive behavior pattern as predictable as the fact that a maple tree will have maple leaves. And Mula had grown into the thing he was among these creatures. His growth had been distorted into the thing it was by their will, degenerate wills about him, augmented into a great hypnotic force by the ancient ray communicators. Here and there through the caverns little groups of these cavern imps lived in a beast-like condition and in some ways they were cunning as a rat, but also as stupid.

It is necessary to explain all this to you so that you will understand what the truckload of escaped captives and myself were up against in making contact. As the truck and trailer came to a Y in the cavern roads I would tell the driver to "turn left" and immediately another voice in his ear would say "no, turn right!" It was the cavern imps at play; a procedure as instinctive to them as a rabbit's jump is to a rabbit. So it took many hours and I was a sleepless nervous wreck before the trailer job finally pulled up to my position.

Out of it poured a dozen job-seeking chorus girls and a half-dozen electrical and radio engineers - Mula's two desires, it seemed.

Most of them would not be missed for months as they had told their friends they were leaving to take a job in another city. How simple it was to fool surface people!

Swiftly I explained the set-up and showed the whole mess with the huge eye. How long we lived depended entirely on whether our surface education should prove better at getting the most out of the old weapons or whether the cavern dwellers' lifelong experience with the profound mechanisms would be too much for us. Already I could feel the far watch rays picking at my brain with tiny needle cutters though immediately I swung the eye in search of attackers. The sensation was gone and no way of knowing

1235

where to look next.

I realized that these apparently idiotic little people of the underworld had an immense potentiality for damage in their experience with reading the mind and their knowledge of the three dimensional geography of the endless caverns. The multihead effect inherent in the use of any telepathic appartus gave them immense mental facility while they used the apparatus; too, parasitically they used any brain with which they were in contact. Paradoxically, this habit did not make them more intelligent; just more aware of danger and harder to handle in conflict.

Their weaknesses were a monkey-like stupidity and the meanness which sat forever in their faces making them hate each other and every living thing.

I SAW, in distant caverns, their little forms racing toward us to get at nearer ray mechanisms and blot us out. Or, what was more likely, capture us for the torture which was one of their pleasures. Of pleasure rays they had almost none. Mula had appropriated most of them or taken parts which rendered them useless. I picked off dozens of them, and as I swept the inumerable galleries with the eye ray, I saw several racing the other way. They did not care for any more argument with me.

Meanwhile the engineers swarmed over the vast machine at which I sat, marveling at its construction. All the working parts were sealed in an air-tight sheath of gold-colored metal; the thing was indestructible except by violence.

One of them, a big red-headed fellow who was an automotive engineer named MacCarthy, climbed to the huge seat beside me. Several of the women were there watching Mula's entertainment on the screen.

"That's him, eh?" said MacCarthy open-mouthed at his first glimpse of Mula's generous folds and ripples. "My would-be employer. If he's not absolutely the most bloated 'pollutocrat' I ever saw I'll eat my hat."

"Yes," I answered, "and any minute he's apt to figure out what to do to get rid of us. Get on your toes, man!"

"Well, it seems quite an apparatus you've got here. I

don't believe in it, mind, but you can't argue with your own eyes. It must have a lot of uses other than peek-a-boo on the neighbors - it's so devilish big. One of those uses should solve our problem. But right now I'm mighty hungry. It couldn't just roll out a few loaves of bread, could it?"

I passed around my pack-load of concentrated food. It was supposed to last me six weeks but they made short work of the best part of it. I dispatched three of the men to my cache at the hole at which I had entered, for food. The rest of us set to work on the banks of levers and buttons that surrounded the huge seat and screen, trying different combinations to see what happened. And plenty happened.

From a scoop-like opening at one side, green globes the size of footballs began to emerge. From another opening a whirring and clattering issued. I was sure something was broken but after a time a strange looking mechanism emerged from the opening with a shiny new appearance like a Christmas bicycle. I stood looking at it wondering what on earth it was when it got up, walked toward me on four legs. The girls screamed and began to run and I was not far behind them. But MacCarthy stood his ground. As the machine came up to him it stopped and a round hole in the top of it began to emit words of a deep, rich, human quality.

The robot was a four-foot cylinder standing erect on four short jointed legs. Only one of these legs moved at a time but very rapidly so that the robot moved at a good walking pace and swayed hardly at all. From the top of the cylinder hung three quite long arms. About the top part of the cylinder were a dozen small apertures covered by fine wire grids. What they were all for I don't know, but the robot, by its own behavior was well equipped with senses.

"God," said MacCarthy, "it's a robot. Now what will we do with a robot?"

I HAD an idea. I called to MacCarthy. "Take it a little distance away, if you can. I'll turn the eye on it and see what its insides are doing."

MacCarthy extended his hand as one would to a child and the robot took hold of his big red paw and followed him

## THE HIDDEN WORLD

away. I swung the huge eye down upon it and instantly I heard its machanical thought answering my own.

"When you need food I will get it," it said in abstract thought. "When you sleep, I will watch. When there is work, I will do it. What do you wish of me?"

Just how much could this robot think was what puzzled me. I soon learned, for the thought of the robot answered my unconscious question.

"I can think as well as a wild animal times three," he seemed to say. Anyway, some multiple of a natural animal's thought was what he meant.

What the green globes were for was a question that had bothered me since their appearance. The robot heard this question in my mind, released MacCarthy's hand, went to the growing pile of glistening rounds, picked up one and mounted the stairs to the seat bearing the globe. With one metal finger he poked a hole in its transluscent shell and held it to my mouth. I tasted it and an ecstacy of flavor spread through me. It was the nectar of the Gods, put up in flexible glass. I whooped, waved the green thing at MacCarthy and the girls.

"It's canned!" I shouted. "Drink up. It's on the house!"

"What a house!" I heard MacCarthy say.

Then the robot sat down beside me, took the controls of the eye from my hands. There was nothing I could do about it; he was built of that metal than which there is no tougher that I have ever found. Methodically the robot swung the eye in ever-widening circles, looking - looking. I watched the screen. The robot saw one of the skinny Hobloks. Under the robot's long metal fingers the thing leaped into center focus. The robot seemed to pause in bewilderment. It was not what he expected to see, it was plain. But the Hoblok was also at a ray mechanism watching us. The robot took perhaps ten seconds to read the thought in the Hoblok's mind, then pressed a stud. The Hoblok rolled over, apparently dead.

The robot continued his sweeping search in ever-widening circles. But I was worried about Mula. Perhaps the robot would - no, it was too much to expect. I tapped the robot's

1238

metal top, pointed in Mula's direction. Obediently he swung the eye as indicated, much quicker and more easily than I myself could. I waved my hand to indicate farther and farther and far as it was, Mula shortly appeared in the screen. I could hear the robot's mechanical mind as he saw Mula's muchness centered on the screen when a blaze of light and deafening sound thundered into our faces. I felt myself falling; knew no more.

I CAME to with my head in the lap of Fanny de Moina, a minature edition of Margie Hart who had fallen for Mula's ad for females. She was bathing my head with the liquid from one of the green globes and pouring some of it down my throat. Either she was one of the most ravishing creatures on earth or the green fluid had remarkable properties.

"What happened?" I asked weakly.

"MacCarthy said Mula must have used your ray path to conduct a heavy jolt of juice back to you. The robot is still out of commission. MacCarthy says since we don't know how to fix a robot we'll have to make another one. He started the big machine making one. You know, Mr. Manville, I didn't get a chance to thank you for saving us from that overgrown hunk of meat. He is the most unattractive man I ever saw, that Mula." She leaned over and planted a highly satisfactory kiss on me.

"Just to show you I enjoyed being rescued from super fatty," she grinned.

MacCarthy and Murray, a radio engineer, a lean, dark Scot, came up leading a new robot different in no way from the other.

"Meet Joe Robot the second. How do you feel?" asked MacCarthy.

"Like I'd been kicked by a Mula," I countered weakly, "but apparently I'm still in working order. Now listen, you two. Since we can't catch Mula any more we're in plenty of danger. Sooner or later he will get a ray centered on us and that will be the end. We've got to figure what to do in a hurry. Was the big ray injured by Mula's juice?"

## THE HIDDEN WORLD

"Couldn't find anything wrong," answered MacCarthy. "Those things are built plenty strong. What a race they have been!"

Allen, a tall, thin, Southern electrical technician, spoke up, "We've been in a huddle about the mess for a couple of hours while you were unconscious. We can't find an answer. We can't kill Mula with this ray. We can't even look at him any more. It looks inevitable. Sooner or later Mula or the Hobloks will do for us. Even if we run; probably quicker if we run, since this huge ray is our only weapon."

"If we could just talk the language that robot is built to use," I mused aloud.

"There is a chance that there are other beings down here as strong or more so than Mula," I went on. "But how to find them or get any help out of them -" I didn't finish, for coming up the wide cavern road were the three men I had sent for food. Their coming had been announced by shouts from the girls who spent most of the time at the screen.

"We have news," were their first words.

"We will soon have visitors and please be nice to them. They were nice to us."

They had hardly thrown down their packs and stretched when out of an opening in the side of the cave popped a long car, glided to a halt near us. A door slid open and something emerged. Fanny promptly fainted; the other girls screamed and went into a complicated clinch with each other. The three men who had just arrived advanced toward the creature in welcome. He was a snail - yet, a man. A long, lumpy brown body oozed toward us, and, centaur-like above it rose the head, shoulders and arms of a man. His neck was surrounded by a foot-long frill extending over his shoulders downward. His mouth was very big and toothless; his nose long and prehensile: it quivered and sniffed at us with a curiosity all its own. But his eyes were big and brown and as gentle as a St. Bernard dog's. He did not waste time.

"YOU WILL be surprised to hear me speak English, but I have had contact with surface people before. I

1240

know you are in trouble here. It is safest for you to come with me at once, without more words. Without my hlep you will soon be killed. There is no time for delay. I will explain things to you on the way. Please come now."

Channing, one of the three who had just arrived, spoke up.

"We were talking with him a long time. His name is Hank. There is a horde of them deeper in the earth, but not many are strong enough to stand gravity this near the surface. There are people like ourselves there too; but they have lived there too long to come to the surface. I think he is our best bet. I don't see any harm in him."

I gave the word, really much elated. I picked up Fanny, who was preparing to come out of her faint.

"Let's go, folks," I called. "This is the subway. Can't keep the train waiting!"

The interior of the car contained some thirty seats. We loaded up our scanty supplies; the green globes had become quite a pile and Joe Robot the second was persuaded to carry Joe the first into the car. This procedure much interested Hank, the snail centaur.

"What is the origin of your people?" I asked Hank.

"We have dwelt deep in the earth always," he began. "Our ruler, the immortal Queen Tanitia, has explained that we're a product of the laboratories of the ancient Gods, especially adapted to difficult underworld conditions, and used in pioneering new borings before they were fully equipped with apparatus adapting the deep caverns to other forms of life. Thus we had inherent abilities which enabled us to survive when most men perished, except on the surface."

"Does any of the ancient wisdom still exist?" I asked, my heart in my mouth.

"Yes," he replied, "our Queen is very old. No one knows how old. We have some of their writings which we study."

God! my mission was close to success!

"You have robots," he remarked coming back to the situation at hand. "That is good. I have heard of them."

The car started slowly into the tube. The tube was smooth metal. From the car's top and bottom and sides projected wheels which were in constant pressing contact with the tube sides. The car was motor driven.

"What kind of a motor is this, anyway?" I asked Hank.

"I don't know," he confessed. "It is an antique like most things we use down here. It runs on water. Many of these ancient engines run on water. You put it in, the engine goes, the water disappears. It is all I know."

The car howled along at a tremendous speed. It swayed hardly at all for the projecting wheels held it rigidly in the center of the tube. The tube dropped steadily downward. Hours went by. Mula was far away, I sighed with relief at the thought. I found my weight had become a trifle for the sigh caused me to lift gently in the seat.

The car flashed along through a mammoth city now. It was larger and more beautiful than any of the caverns we had yet seen. The tube in which we had descended had come out into the city cavern in a channel that ran through the city on stilts, like surface elevated trains. The top half of the car was transparent and about us lay the ancient homes of mighty immortal beings lit and tenanted; looking much as it must have when it was young. Across it hummed tiny heliplanes; along the ways, many cars like our own sped. Here and there glided or grouped the snail people, not unlovely once you were used to them. Their head crests glittered irridescently when they moved. Theirs was a gentle purposefulness as there is about a good horse in action. Among them I noticed many human forms like our own though clad in short glittering tunics and with long hair floating. They took prodigious strides when they walked, I noticed.

OUR car glided to a halt before a huge doorway, flanked by snailmen at guard holding, strangely enough, modern rifles.

Hank led us up the inclined plane at a vastly more rapid glide than he had shown us near the surface. He seemed very different down here; his breath slow and even, his eyes gleaming with strength, his frill standing out sharply beautiful, veined like a big flower.

I rose several feet in the air at each step. I weighed little, had a sensation of strength I had never felt before.

We followed Hank's gliding form up the ramp, around a glistening curve of transparent walls through a hallway into a courtroom glittering with lush human life and brilliant with laughing, intelligent young faces. At a desk on a dais at one end of the place lay a woman. She rose as we entered and came swiftly toward us, her hands outstretched in greeting. My heart leaped at sight of her, not so much because of the beauty, but because of the sensation of burning thought that lay on her face.

"We know your troubles," were her words, "because they are similar to that of all surface people and because we have the same troubles everywhere we go except here. Here it is safe and we will help plan a future for you."

Hank bowed low before her.

"Queen Shola, these are the people who escaped from the great hulk Mula, and this is the man who rescued them. His name is Manville."

The Queen extended her hand to me.

"I understand," she said, "that Mula did not enjoy meeting you."

"He did squeak a little about it," I admitted. "How is it that you are so well acquainted with our difficulty?"

"All over the world," answered the Queen, "these caverns extend to within a few miles of the surface and all through the caverns playing and fighting with the ancient mechanisms are the Hobloks and their kind. Mostly they are mean and evil and foolish; but they have been living with the ray equipment for so many centuries that its use has become instinctive with them and many of them are very adept at its various uses. They torment and injure surface people to such an extent that there is little hope for their progress, especially as they are so totally unaware of the evil or its extent. Just as the Hobloks have made Mula a thing of evil, though he was once a vital animal, so do they make of many surface leaders foolish and evil creatures through their

1243

continuous lies and thought tamper.

"They thwart all scientific effort on the surface. They stop every good thing before it becomes a part of surface life. We have often tried to exterminate the creatures, but we have only succeeded in clearing a few of these deep earth cities of their influence. In the far distance they spy on us still. The ancient wave rays at which they sit are too powerful for us to overcome.

"If we try to make a clean surface place so as to cure some surface life of their influence and bring back the study of the ancient science through the study of the ancient machines, our efforts come to nothing because we can never get enough of the old ray positions in our hands to protect ourselves fully. Our men become, in a short time, foolish or insane from the needling they get from unreachable old rays.

"It seems impossible that intelligent men could not overcome these foolish Hobloks. But when they turn on the old rays it gives them immense awareness; they are super destructive. We have not succeeded in freeing any surface life of them."

"You are the ruler of this great city?" I asked Queen Shola.

"I am just a sub-ruler; I have been appointed to rule over the humans of the city. The real ruler is a very old and immortal being whom we seldom see. You will be taken before her presently."

"Immortal?" I queried.

"I know already why you came to the underworld. We have been taking records of your thought since before you arrived. You came to learn the secret of immortality. There is no reason," she went on, "why you should not succeed."

"THESE snail men seem very intelligent," I observed.

"There is a reason for their intelligence," she affirmed. "You see, the potentialities of mind-reading apparatus are immense. The multihead effect alone contains enough power to pull the whole human race into a wonderful new way of life. We have developed this side of ray work quite a bit. You see, if we are in mental contact, my brain's questions are answered automatically by yours, if it possesses the answer. So that we are actually much more intelligent than two people not in contact, are we not? We are as intelligent as the number of brain cells active in your head multiplied by the number in my head which is something like a thousand times as intelligent as two ordinary people not in contact. We have developed this principle - called the Multihead principle - into mind teams containing many hundreds of specialists, each brain trained to use all the resources of all the other brains. The result is a group of men perhaps a billion times as intelligent as an ordinary human. Would you like to talk to someone trained in such a school?"

I looked at her lovely, quizzical face and suddenly realized I was talking to a person as far superior to myself as a man is superior to a worm.

"I think I am talking to such a person." The simplicity and enormity of the multihead principle had floored me.

"The multi-head principle is one thing we tried very hard to get surface people to adopt. But they listened to the idiotic tamper of our Hoblok opposition and fearfully refused to work on telepathic apparatus. In some ways you are still medieval, you surface men. This principle is one reason Mula gets along so well - hundreds of minds are slaves to him and always in contact. His mind uses them parasitically."

"They do have a reactionary attitude toward some types of new things, it is true," I agreed.

"You don't know how hard we have tried to make them able to be of use to us. We are in constant bitter warfare with the insane Hobloks. Come, I will show you. The mind-record workers tell me you are wholly trustworthy."

The rest of my party never missed me. A group of uniformed officers surrounded the girls, some of whom, like Fanny de Moina, were real beauties. The six engineers were likewise surrounded by a bevy of underworld charm and MacCarthy's red face was wreathed in grins. I guessed he was describing the expansive Mula; I could hear them laughing.

QUEEN SHOLA led me into an adjoining apartment. Here the walls were a series of television screens on each of which a scene of struggle was taking place. On the center of each, some far distant ancient giant of a ray generator, topped by a Hoblok, sent vast streams of energy toward the receiver. These were met and neutralized by great black shorter rays somewhere between. In the lower part of the screen could be seen the uniformed head and shoulders of a snail man, his peculiar webbed hands manipulating the defense mechanisms. At some of the rays were humans, also in uniform.

"This particular war is ten years old," said Queen Shola. "You see, the ancient rays were so built and situated that they could not successfully fight against each other so that no revolution could take place by their use. At the same time they are so strong and well constructed that no weapon our weak modern minds can devise will subdue them. It is a premeditated deadlock so designed by the ancient Godrace. The Hobloks, of course, cannot understand this and try to fight with them; and, perforce, we must fight back with the ancient stationary ray. It is all extremely stupid and repetitive, but so far we have not found the answer. We are defeated by the brilliance of the ancient minds which built and placed the ancient rays as a check on any attempt to dominate their life. Do you follow?"

"I begin to understand," I mused aloud, "why Hobloks are such a menacing nuisance, yes."

"You see," she went on, "when you grow a large alligator you have created a greater menace to your limbs. When a Hoblok steps into an ancient ray operator's seat he becomes a much larger bit of deviltry though just as stupid and undesirable."

"Multihead stupidity is still stupidity."

"Exactly," she answered. "That is what war is - stupidity multiplied by a force. And that is what Hoblok ray is - stupidity multiplied by titanic ancient force. Thus all

## THE HIDDEN WORLD

our brilliance and knowledge of growth and science is neutralized by the Hoblok multiple - titanic idiocy."

"They are charming creatures. How did they get that way?" I asked.

"Endless centuries of secret parasitism on surface people have given them a sort of leech-soul! They never learned to use the growth generators or synthetic food machines of the ancients, but they did learn to use the view rays and some of the weapons. They used them so long that the worn-out machines give off a detrimental emanation which contributed to the degeneration of the original flesh pattern into the leech-like form of flesh it is. They are in truth a different form of life: more akin to such parasitic creatures than to man."

"You certainly confirm my suspicions on the matter. Have you tried bribery, turning them against each other?"

"They have so little organization it is not hard. We have had some success in that line. But in reality we are fighting the ancient mechanisms and when they get hold of one, they live in it. It becomes their life and they are unapproachable then, as you learned yourself when you argued with Mula. You could have held out for years there if you kept careful watch. Mula himself is checkmated and made the thing he is by these creatures. So he amuses himself with torture and waits for death. His thought is now a fixed pattern as is theirs.

"You will find many such products of growth-force generators in the underworld. Our own ruler is one. But she is different, younger; and we ourselves have worked with and renewed the growth-force mechanism till there is little danger of unbalanced growth."

"YOU mentioned that Mula's thought is fixed pattern as is the Hobloks. Will you explain?" I asked Shola.

"When we look at an insect like a spider or a wasp," she replied, "we see only an exact repetition of all other spiders or wasps, just as leaves on a tree are like the other leaves on the same tree. Their whole lives are exact repetitions of the lives of all other spiders and wasps of the

1247

same kind. This is also almost true of men: they are merely repetitions of each other and the past and the whole future of their lives is predictable from the past. Only when the intake of growth material is greater than the intake of detrimental material for long periods is there any growth into new ways of life. There have been many Mulas in the past of the caverns, and they have almost all followed the same course as the present Mula. Some parts of the thing are ritualistic and traditional: the red-horned masks, the torture - all are repetitions of ancient times. Mula adapted them to his own uses, which have also turned out to be the same."

"This conflict is endless, then?"

"It has been going on for untold centuries in these caverns with infinite slight variations, of course, but always the same theme: intelligent people trying to rebuild the ancient wisdom and way of life always thwarted by the degenerate creatures who are, as you have seen, wholly destructive. The ancient mechanisms do not wear out, so the war needs no vast supply of weapons. There are always more of the creatures and even if there were no intelligent people to fight, they would still fight each other."

We strolled back into the great throne room. Fanny de Moina ran up to us and took my arm.

"Look," she said in amazement, "I thought I could dance!"

A welcome dance had been organized. Under the very slight gravity these people had evolved a most complicated and acrobatic dance routine wholly impossible to those not accustomed to weighing so little. We could only watch, and the envious eyes of the chorus girls, probably as good dancers as surface earth produced, subtly amused me. The flying, graceful limbs and easy, almost floating movements of young bodies whose feet only touched the floor at intervals of seconds were an infinitely finer picture of the dance than I had ever seen before.

The Queen sent a page to summon the rest of the newly arrived surface people.

"The ruler has sent for you all."

## THE HIDDEN WORLD

WE ENTERED an elevator. We came out on the roof of a tower which overlooked the whole city of Loer. Like a pent-house garden the roof was adorned with living trees and plants and was bathed in a rich, warm light more pleasant than any sun. In the center was a round building. As we approached it, soft invisible emanations exquisitely stimulating ran over us, reading us and at the same time waking us to an intense sense of pleasure, of anticipation. Before the door was a statue of many-breasted Tanit; not by surface sculptors, but something by the ancients. Its beauty was indescribable, unthinkable, in truth. Their art always leaves a man gasping. We entered softly.

She sat in one of the ancient god seats. It was not too big. If earth has anything approaching the ancient Gods in strength, and in beauty, she is it. She was very old, we knew; but time had left only a wise crinkling about her eyes and humor marks at her lips. Her skin was soft and fresh and within her perfect body one could sense the strength. About her were several snail men and a trio of very young maidens sat at her feet, one of whom softly strummed a harp.

About her played a greenish ray. It said to my nerves all things that nerves need to hear, and all the things nerves are pleased to feel.

Her hair was flame red; her skin that white that often goes with red hair. Her eyes were very dark and brooding, yet very welcome to look at. One did not turn away but looked deeper and saw a friend. On her shoulder sat a crested bird and at her feet lounged a huge lion-like dog. Her feet were sandaled; her gown a severe transparent Grecian drape. On her large breast some huge emeralds glittered. She was woman - all wise, desiring woman-flesh and she was beautiful. The force in her gaze was tremendous; one could not help desiring her.

She talked and her voice filled the room with woman-sound and the sensing of a mind too big to comprehend. Queen Shola swiftly translated into English.

"You will have to stay with us a while. The ways to the surface are not at present open to us. We will try to make your stay pleasant and of value to you and to us."

We talked a while, but our audience was disappointing in that we had, in truth, little to say to a mind as deep and capable as hers. And we all felt this. But she was curious as to conditions on the surface and very interested in our answers to her questions. She was very disappointed as to the condition of science in general. We were given some refreshments; stimulating fluids of several kinds were served and little nut-shaped sweetmeats. We were somehow ill at ease at our own lack of life and strength.

Presently we returned to the lower floors. Some of the girls tried to join in the dance and did not do so badly. Presently we were shown to several chambers equipped with modern-looking beds.

WHEN I awoke Queen Shola herself had come with a page bearing a tray of food.

"And this is the food you people eat that makes your young people so uniformly well-constructed, so very generally beautiful!"

"The ancients had vast greenhouses lit by artificial heating rays. We have repaired some of them and learned to raise all our food down here. These whom you think young people are, some of them, hundreds of years old. We have almost conquered age. We have learned to read the old books, many of them still exist; and age was a subject they were very interested in. They are very hard to understand but our multihead teams can manage to get the meaning from their simpler books for young people.

"Could I, O Queen, could I see some of those ancient books?"

She smiled, and all the graciousness a vast mind was capable of lay on her face.

"Why not?" she said simply.

This was a booklover's entrance into Paradise. My knees knocked like a prospective bridegroom's. The vast, intricately worked metal doors slowly opened as we approached. The stacks extended as far as the eye could reach in any direction. The books were of metal and most of them four to five feet square. The hours fled and I could not tear myself away. Both the Queen and little Fanny de Moina had gone away, perhaps understanding what this meant to me.

At last I held the book for which I searched on my knees. Even there it was too heavy. The pages were covered with those strange letters, a language to which few surface men but myself held the key. Laboriously I translated the pages, one by one. Here it was: under the symbol for Life - L - followed by the symbol for "on" followed by a symbol which meant to the Nth power - meant infinity. Swiftly I wrote those blazing words which would change the life of the world to something worth having if I could bring them back to surface man.

## The Formula "Live On"

TO LIVE successfully is to conquer life's problems. This can only be done by changing the conditions of your life to eliminate the detrimental factors. Thus the influx of detrimental energy flows must be excluded, while the intake of beneficial energy must be increased. To prolong life indefinitely, even under deadly suns - a super-dense metal is particularly useful. This is true for this important reason - disintegrant energy cannot exist except it have an integrated particle to feed on - just as fire cannot exist without fuel. A beneficial force flow is a ray which is rich in the ultimate end product of disintegrance - energy ash. Take the most dense metal you can obtain - and force an energy flow through it at high pressure; those bits of matter which keep disintegrance alive will be excluded by the density of the metal, just as ashes fall through a grate and leave the burning fire above. The life-giving ash of energy from which all matter is reintegrated is the product of such a device. A flow rich in energy ash causes an immediate increase in the mental function to an amazing degree, as well as stimulates and causes a new growth - a more powerful and intelligent being is created immediately by subjection to such a flow. Immortality can be achieved by excluding all persistently disintegrant particles from the whole intake of the animal. This is the path which our race took to greatness, to the conquest of space,

1251

to life everlasting in the darkness of space.

Such metals can be obtained floating free in space, the product of gravitic space storm vortexes. These metals form the heart of our most important mechanisms - the growth-force generators.

THE secret of immortality! It lies in "empty" space! Now I, and you, have the secret of the metal shield that can make us live forever - and with two ways to construct it: By scientific work on magnetic vortex flows, utilizing ex-disintegrance to "pack" ordinary metal with energy ash - or, by sending men out into space itself in space ships!

Scientists - rocket men - listen to me! This is all true! Work at it; I have neither the ability nor the money. I have given you the formula. I have done my part. Do yours, for God's sake, while I still live!

Harte Manville.

# THE HIDDEN WORLD

1253

# THE HIDDEN WORLD

1254

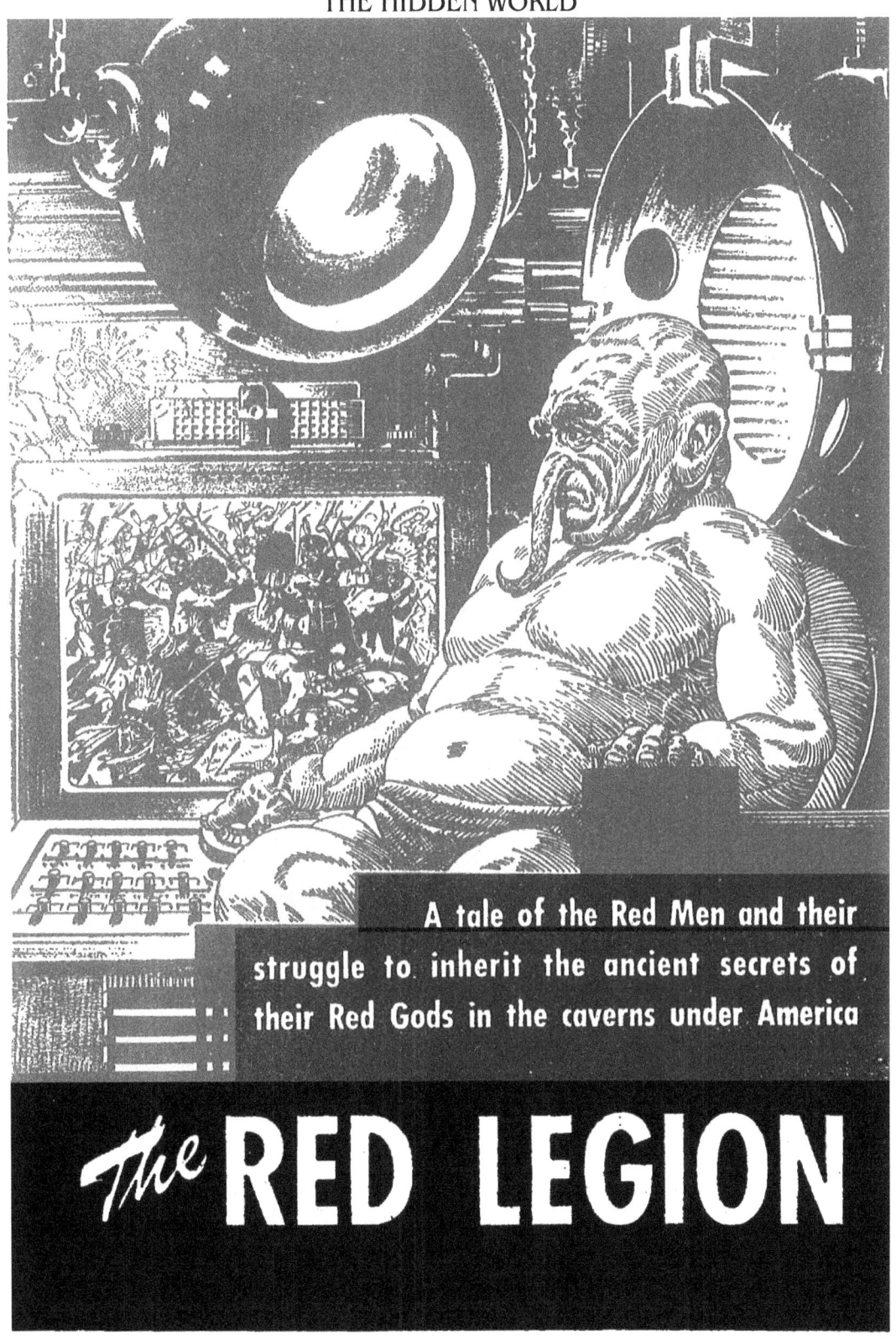

# THE HIDDEN WORLD
## By RICHARD S. SHAVER

### FOREWORD:

OUT OF THE hideous mire of futility, out of the lost, near-forgotten glories of the Indian Race, comes again a striving - even into the present!

Out of vanished power and Empire, comes today the word of the Red Men: "We live on, and we know. We will again be great . . ."

Under Death Valley; under Butte, Montana; under many Western states; out of the green hell of South America; out of Yucatan; of Central America; and out of Mexico - come many reports that there are large areas of the Elder caves held by Indians. These areas the white monopoly of all antique ray people, for all their mocking and their vaunting and suppression, are unable to overcome.

There, still today, something of an ancient art and wisdom vastly different in every way from that of the white-dominated ray caverns survives - untouched by the corruption and blight of modern ray evils.

There, too, survives that savagery and worship of strange Gods characterized by the Aztec ceremony of cutting the heart out of a living victim - and offering it to their "God."

There, too, survives something best characterized by the poem of Longfellow - "Hiawatha," known to all of you. That something that lives in all men, but which many Indians still call "The Great Spirit."

There, too, survives a white and pitiful thing that once was red and courageous and strong. Other things that once were men, are no longer enough like men to be so called.

I am going to tell you a story of the struggles of the Red Men in the caverns, those who have preserved their courage and their intelligence, and their noble efforts to make of the ancient secrets a powerful tool for the rehabilitation of the Red Race.

It is historic fact that whole tribes of Indians mysteriously vanished without trace before the advance of the white man. It is not so generally know that they disappeared, in many

1256

cases, into the fearful vastnesses of the labyrinthine mysteries of the Elder Race's former home.

The traveler in the white-dominated portions of the caverns today finds the marks of their Indian cooking fires against the walls of polished and carved walls, the water jars and pottery, the crude wall paintings, sometimes overlaying the glorious work of the Elder Race. These things they have left all through the American caverns - and they are things left by Indians of culture completely the same as the Red Men of Revolutionary times. For many tribes of Indians of those times when they fled ever westward from civilization (as we whites call our social order) knew of the God caverns and the tremendous things they contained. But they apparently did not know how to use these things.

How much they did know of the operation and use of the terrific power of the Elder machines we cannot know, but we do know that for two centuries no "spiritualist" "sent his spirit" into the "spirit world" without an "Indian guide." That this ever-present "Indian-guide" in all spiritualist doings was the descendant of those same tribes who fled into the eternal darkness and fearful wonder of the underworld to escape the white man's massacre of the Indian is very plain to anyone who knows anything of the history and the customs of the caverns. That they did not use the weapons, but only the telaug, is easily understood when one knows of the Elder Race custom of sealing all weapons against casual search; within great vaults that are not casually found by the ignorant.

To those who know of the trickery and deceit always practised by the underworld peoples to hide the existence of their homes, this Indian guide to the "spiritualists" is very recognizable as the Indian race in the caverns hiding themselves with an easily committed lie. That they should assist white spiritualists at their "seances" seems to furnish a picture of their inability to find a practical use for their time in the mysterious world of darkness. To one who has seen what the Indian of the caverns has become from the effects of lack of sunlight and air and proper food, one can understand why the Red Men of the caves have not been a

1257

very potent force in American history.

That these "Indian guides" are a phenomena never encountered much of late years speaks volumes to one who knows of the constant warfare and the fragile margin on which life persists in the caves.

They, the original Red Men, the original tribes who entered the darkness, must have been recently persecuted and pursued and killed until they are no longer there in any numbers.

But, one hears from the West that still the Red Men struggle for life in the western and southern states and are succeeding in holding large areas against the modern white monopolists: those same suppressors and secretives who keep the mighty wisdom of the Elder Work in the caverns from modern men of the surface.

This story is of that struggle: to give you these heretofore unwritten pages of the secret (in this case quite recent) history of our earth.

## CHAPTER I

### Death Speaks to the Legion

THE voice, out of the dark silence of the night, had said: "Every day one member of your Red Legion shall die."

Eonee Lane had paid no attention, for a voice in the night out of nowhere he knew could be anything. Could be his nerves, imagination, or the mischeivous and mad ones of the unseen below.

But, one by one, the men of the Red Legion about Butte, Montana - had died!

One! Every day - one more! One every day! Why?

So hard it had been, building the Legion of the Loyal Red Men. . . .

Out of the hideous mire of futility that had consumed the Red Men;

Out of the miserable remnants of his race he had welded together this striving, active, educated and aware and able

## THE HIDDEN WORLD

force of young men, seen it grow in numbers and in skill at the secret role they must play;

Out of a defeated and complacent nothing he had built, through the years, a strong and united spirit in the sons of his race, men who knew what terrific power might yet be won by them.

Now, suddenly, the unseen and mysterious underworld forces that had helped him so long; that had caused the Red Legion to grow almost miraculously to become a strong secret power through all the west; had turned instead into a destroying blight about Montana.

Every day some Indian friend's death was reported in the Butte daily news. No one noticed these deaths, apparently, but Lane. So far as he knew no one else had heard the voices in the night mocking the Red Legion and prophesying a daily death for its members; a prophecy that came true every day!

Each death was one strong son the ancient blood who had joined the legion.

Lane bent his black head into his arms, his strong back slumped over his desk. He felt old and beaten, though he was but thirty-eight.

The sun, shining redly out of the west into his wide office window, outlined the letters: "E. Lane and J. Stevens - Attorneys."

\* \* \*

ANOTHER, of very different appearance from surface man, but of the ancient blood that can still produce such vigorous fighters as Jim Thorpe and in the past has produced its share of Hiawathas - many, many men, now forgotten whose deeds rang then in the ears of all men on the American continent - yes, another of that fierce and ancient blood knew too of the deaths. Johnny Ahahne, his name, and he knew too, why these deaths occurred.

Johnny Ahahne, for the past few months, was reduced to bearing burdens. Before that, he had been a high-placed, somewhat lazy, member of the ruling caste of the tribe of Indians who held the caverns under Montana. They had more wealth and more power than most white men ever dream of

1259

possessing. They had, too, an ancient inability to make much use of the wealth and power - through lack of desire.

Johnny Ahahne, Indian bearer, glanced at the notice, printed in, to him nearly unreadable English words. Carries not Delivered on Deep Levels. He adjusted his tump strap, straightened his lean muscular legs under the 150-pound pack of luxury items from the surface. Silently he thanked the Great Spirit, and the mighty invisible serpent who had given his brothers courage to face death rather than submit to carrying the heavy packs to the deepest lower levels. Now they were not required to travel beyond their strength. Inwardly Johnny realized that this leniency was exercised only in order to keep them alive and available.

As Johnny plodded off into the dimly-lit boring his hand slid into his loin cloth, fumbled for an instant with a folded bit of paper. His brothers on the surface must know of what had come to pass. Of the fate that had overtaken the ancient, secret and aloof strength of the Red Men of under-earth. The Red Legion had been their favorite project for the future. They must be told; those red brothers on the surface. They must be warned of what had happened down here.

Two miles from the "Express Office" Johnny looked about carefully. Then he reached with his mind's awareness for the ionizing of any watchray upon him. At last, convinced he was unobserved, he slipped the little paper out of his loin cloth and slid it into a tiny unmarked crevice in the ancient hardened rock of the wall. Silently, unthinkingly, his mind a careful blank, Johnny Ahahne plodded on his long carry into the dark.

He did not love the white European ray people. This Da Sylva woman who had taken over the Elder caverns under Butte, Montana, was a cruel creature, and her gang was worse, when possible. When the short, bloody, decisive battle was over, there was left alive but a few hundred of the red warriors. For them was designated the labor, the dirty jobs no one else wanted, and the working of the ancient mines. Johnny, as so many of his ancestors in the past, cursed his heathen curses on all white men and moved on into the ever-dark.

1260

## THE HIDDEN WORLD

But the little paper did not remain in the unnoticeable slot in the hardened rock of the ancient cavern wall. An hour later another bearer paused, reached with his mind to sense the ionizing of the watch rays, looked at the age-old dust to watch the furry bristling that tattled on the electric flows of a watch ray. The bristling dust died into quiescence, it was but the wind of his slight movement. He reached into the slot, took the paper. Many days he had looked into the secret place, found nothing. Today there was a message. He knew it was for the red brothers on the surface - those who knew.

By such stages the paper finally reached the surface. In the overalls of a red-skinned cowhand the paper traveled toward Butte.

* * *

IN Butte, Lane's partner, Jack Stevens, parked his Buick coupe near the long-limbed animal from the Ranch of the Elder Twin. Stevens stood by his car absently filling his pipe, his tall, spare, wide shouldered figure well dressed in dark gray, well-pressed worsted. His aquiline, high cheekboned face was expressionless. Only the glitter of his heavy-lidded black eyes betrayed his intent awareness. Only the Indians who belonged to the Red Legion knew that the Ranch of the Elder Twin was built over an ancient Entrance to the Elder World; a world that only the Indians of this part of the west knew existed. Only a few of the Indians knew that the Elder Twin was a living God who inhabited the deeper caverns of the Elder World. Only a very few of them fully realized the tremendous nature of the secret covered by that low-built ranch house.

Stevens stood still a long time, eyeing that rangy bay horse from the ranch. Johnny Ahahne's voice had told him in the night there would be a message - written - that he could depend on; that would be no fake by some imp of the dark.

The cowhand came out of the store, swung into the saddle, moved down the wide street. Stevens bent, picked up the paper. The Red Legion had contacted the unseen.

# THE HIDDEN WORLD

SHORTLY Stevens entered the office that bore his and Lane's names on the window.

Lane looked up at his partner, but did not move from his slumped, discouraged position at the big desk. Stevens tossed the still-folded paper in front of Lane.

Lane's dark eyes quickened. He picked up the paper, unfolded it jerkily. On it was a series of pictographs, readable only to a few Indians; or to a student who knew the lesser languages of the Indians. They are few.

As Lane pored over the message, two men came into the office. They were cowhands of Indian blood from another ranch near Butte, the Barred Y. Lane passed the message to one of these men, sat watching his face as he deciphered the near-forgotten symbols. One by one more and more men filed into the office. Lane knew by the man's face that he was not wrong, that the message meant exactly what he had read it to mean. There was no mistake. The Red Legion was doomed if it stayed here.

The Brotherhood of the Unseen had given the sign.

THERE were now some thirty dark, hawk-faced young men gathered in the big office room. Ten of them took seats about a broad oak table. The rest stood in the rear, in the shadows, watching stolidly with emotionless eyes - they were all Indian today. That Stevens and Lane were names taken to avoid white prejudice against the Indian origin of the men only themselves knew, for no one else cared. There were many of Indian blood. Lane took the chair at the head of the table. But he did not sit in it. He stood, face upraised, hands outstretched, both hands with palms upward, fingers extended. Solemnly he intoned,

"Eemeeshee, our great Breath-Master, twin brother of the Wolf of the Skys, we beg your guidance and your blessing upon us. Each day for one month, one of us has died. The voices have told us that this will continue until all who know the Elder Secret are dead. Will you, we implore you, ancient one, come from your dreams and aid us?"

Into the stodgy law-office stole an awesome breath out of Time, a breath from the far past of the glories of the Red

Race. And into each dark expressionless face of the Indians gathered there came a brightening; a hope. Their ancient God lived. He had answered. He had not answered their prayers since their fathers were young men. All had felt his mighty breath stirring primevally in the dusty law office.

\* \* \*

MANY hundreds of miles away, and many miles underground - a living being turned slowly from his vast crystalline instrument panel. It was good to hear his name "Eemeeshee" again upon the lips of men. Once, long ago, the red men had plagued him nigh to death with their prayers; he had shut off the listening electric ears of the huge machine that brought to him the thoughts of men up in the sunlight. Time had slipped by in the strange dream life he led. He had turned on the great magic ear again, and had heard but one voice questing him from among the many thought voices intermingling, the voice of Eonee Lane of Butte, Montana. Delicately he had sought with the directive dial needles for the source of that thought, and had almost brought the scene in the law office into his screens. But it was too far; he had given up after a time. Eemeeshee was not industrious.

Mayhap you have seen ancient Indian drawings of their gods floating in the air over the heads of their rulers. Horrible appearing things, with foot-long noses and wide ears, like an elephant, gross bodies and peculiar looking limbs. Those artists were not liars, for ...

Eemeeshee's nose was over a foot long. The end of his nose turned up in a sickle from the weird growth that had distorted him - due to the peculiar rays of the ancient machine in which he lived. Eemeeshee's head was vast and horrible too, and his body was a mass of flesh too vast to worry about any more and Eemeeshee hardly thought of his appearance. It was not important. Few things were important to Eemeeshee.

The growth rays of the machine in which he sat, and which had kept him alive through the slow drag of the centuries while he dreamed away his too numerous lifetimes, had made him grow unaccountably in some ways -

1263

in others not at all. His face was seamed and lined, yet the flesh was soft and pink as a baby's flesh. He belonged to a race unknown to surface man!

Long ago, his ancestors had found that certain machines of the God caverns, if one remained within them, kept one alive century after century. And the living in them was very pleasant, too.

The magic of the Gods who had built them gave to one endless dreams at the touch of a button. Endless dreams of love, of Goddess-like women, of glory and war and conquest. In fact, one had only to think when one had punched the dream button, and whatever one wished became a reality in a dream more vivid than ever was reality.

That family had few children. The dream life does not make for that. But some they did have, and servants by the score. So that wherever one of the great living machines was to be found, there was found one of the strange and ancient dwellers within. The men of the surface once worshipped these invisible listening ears, for they might be persuaded to do great magic for one, if one asked them correctly - and frequently.

SOFTLY Eemeeshee turned from the listening place, his heavy breathing soughing in the augmentive apparatus like a great wind. If he had had the rays turned upward, he would have been heard like a great spirit of the winds, breathing in the skies, and that was why he was called the Breath-Master, because he did not shut off the intake of the augmentor, and was always heard breathing. Perhaps he did not know it could be shut off. He turned on the searching eye rays, looked about up on the slowly darkening surface in the evening calm. All was different up there than it had once been, long ago when he had watched the red men fight their wars. Their war-whoops had once been given in conflict even down in the cavern world. Long centuries had Eemeeshee sat, and his father had sat there before him. Eemeeshee did not know if he was a God or not, but he supposed it must be so; had not men worshipped the Eemeeshees for an age?

## THE HIDDEN WORLD

Eemeeshee wondered a bit where all the Indians had gone, and who these pale people with their ugly machinery and railroads and square houses might be who had taken over all the land above of late. He had not paid much attention to the upper world for a long time. Time didn't matter much anyway. Old Eemeeshee did not care greatly about the actual world. To him it was like an unwanted program on the televisor; too commercial to listen to: like the radio in the house of a person who does not approve of the commercially raucous sounds it emits. Eemeeshee seldom looked at the upper world. He only half believed in it, anyway. Dreams were much more real, and far more beautiful. The dream world into which his dream device plunged him was vastly more satisfying. Was it not more vived, more full of sweet sound and pleasant sensation and mightier people and vastly stronger love? Eemeeshee was not in love with the world of the actual above his head.

Eemeeshee seldom talked to mere men. There were too many interesting characters in the library of wire film which furnished his dream mech with material. Too, the dream mech made these people real and when one asked them questions or talked to them, they answered. They were vastly more pleasing than mere people of the world over head. Certainly the dream world was one to live in; it rewarded him for every effort with an infinitude of pleasures.

There were few living men who really knew if Eemeeshee was a reality or a legend from the past. One of these was the chief of his servants. He kept the things of the world from interfering with Eemeeshee's pleasures. There was Saba, the keeper of his women. Like all the great of the cavern world, Eemeeshee was well supplied with women, but he did not bother them greatly. They lived altogether in the women's quarters. Under Saba's clever rule they kept busy and to themselves. They were not important, and to Eemeeshee, Saba was like a daughter; a daughter whom he protected from the ugly world of reality. It was better not to know how worthless it was.

In truth, he badly neglected the lives of the people around

him, who waited on him hand and foot and even loved him a little. But, then, Eemeeshee was only a forgotten legend, and their lives only a reflection of the glories that had been the life of the caverns when the Red Man was a **power** on the earth above and had sent always young blood down into the ancient darkness to keep things alive and pulsing.

There was still a lot of life in Eemeeshée's great body. But it was a life that was not greatly interested in itself or in anyone else, either. Eemeeshee was a victim of the greatest vice on earth, the record-mech dreams of the Gods, and his practical knowledge of life and his machines or anything important to an ordinary man was in truth elementary - extremely so.

## CHAPTER II

### The Red Men Meet

FAR off from the hidden, forgotten place where the old one cogitated the vast mysteries of an existence he had never bothered to understand, the meeting of the Red Legion in the Law Offices of Eonee Lane and Jack Stevens began.

Stevens sat down, and Lane continued standing. In his hand was the paper Stevens had given him. He began to talk - low-pitched college English.

"A thing we have long suspected has been confirmed. The rule in the hidden places under Montana is no longer in the hands of the Red Men. A swift surprise attack gave the power into the hands of foreign white conspirators. They have deluded us into thinking no change took place.

Lane handed the paper to the man seated next. The man looked at the paper a long time. It was not easy for him to decipher the Indian pictographs. Finally he nodded, passed the paper on to the next. The paper made the circuit of the room, returned to Stevens.

"For you fellows who can't read the ancient writing of our fathers - the pictograph come from one John Ahahne. Once he was a high-placed warrior of the tribe in power below. Now he is reduced to bearing burdens on his back for the white interlopers. The Indian has lost another great battle with the white man. These European ray people who have again begun the ancient battle against the red man, have wiped out the friendly white ray of the east - and have now turned their attention to the portions held from ancient times by red men."

Stevens stopped, stared moodily at the long table top. Lane's cultured voice went on where Stevens had stopped.

"To the red men of the surface, who are few enough and poor enough as it is - we who have been taken into the ancient secret only because we are few and because our red skins created a bond of sympathy with the red skins of the underworld - this means that to prosper in the future we must remove ourselves from this area to another where the red man still holds the secret caverns against the new threat."

As Lane ceased, one Ace Kitka spoke:

"There have been many deaths of red men whom I know, of late. I have heard voices threatening me with death, saying that each day one Indian dies until there are no more of us in all this area. I have watched the papers, wondered whether the voice in the night spoke true. It did speak true; the red men are being killed by invisible rays. The deaths are usually heart failure, according to the doctor's death certificates. I have decided to leave Montana far behind myself. If you know what is good for you, you will all go from here."

"Several of my intimate friends have died lately," agreed Lane. "They died apparently naturally: one run over by a truck, one of pneumonia, one of a brain hemorrhage. To us who know the power of the ancient machines, we know that these deaths are not accidents - when they are accompanied by threats from the voices. I, too, have heard the voice."

A deep voice from the back of the crowd made itself heard.

"John Ahahne, a voice I have known for many years, always speaks truth. If he has given us warning that this is not a place for red men, it is true. Ill luck will dog us from the enmity of these spiteful newcomers below. They are no longer our friends; our friends are dead. They are masquerading as our friends while they bring about our destruction. You know that almost always the men of the caverns kill those who know the ancient secret of their dwelling place. If these new conquering ray practice that ancient custom of guarding the secret of the rays, we have no choice but to flee - and far."

A CHORUS of voices began to struggle to be heard - agreeing, telling of ill luck and deaths of friends and relatives. Stevens raised a hand.

"That is enough. I see it is true. We have been blind to think the ray people below are still friendly as of old. Let us leave this country, together, all of us, and find a country where the underworld still contains men friendly to us, or some of the ancient ones to protect us."

One Lee Johnson thrust his lean overalled body to the fore of the room.

"The main idea is to go where things are good. Maybe the ray won't talk to us other places, but they may leave us alone. They may even help us get started again."

A FUNERAL caravan of motor cars left Butte the next morning. In the long line of cars were some fifty men, their wives and families. Others were leaving singly for locations of their own choosing. Their belongings were lashed to the sides and tops of the cars. In the hearse was the latest of the dead of the Red Legion. He had died in the night of a "hemorrhage, cause unknown." The white men watched the funeral caravan uncomprehendingly.

"Looks like our Indians are turning gypsy, or something. Funny they'd take all that stuff on a funeral trip. Wonder what the police have to say about it?"

"Guess they got a right to leave if they want to. It's when they decide to stop their troubles will begin. There are a lot of Indian laws that Lane and Stevens know plenty about and they are in that line. Must know what they're doing with these two along. They got a hearse in the line. May be a smart trick to avoid bother with the law, eh?"

1268

## THE HIDDEN WORLD

"Yeh, it's funny so many Indians would get ready for a long trip thataway. They could be taking a dead one to some special place to bury him, I guess."

"Been a lot of Indians dying lately. Nearly every day I read something about a dead Indian. Maybe they're wiser than we think."

"Could be, could be . . ."

"Indians around Butte here have always had a reputation for knowing what's coming next. There's always been something mysterious about it. Never could figure it out. Maybe that is more than a funeral and maybe it ain't. We'll never know. I'll bet a dime we never see those Indians again, though."

Similar conversations could have been heard along the highway leading out of Butte. But nobody thought of asking the Indians what it was all about.

That night, as the long caravan made camp, they dug a grave for Ace Kitka. His weeping wife and two papooses; the solemn faces of the men of the caravans; the grim knowing that the road into the dark deathland gaped for all of them in this land of the white man just as it had for their ancestors was a terrible thing. To know that every day one of them must die . . . Why? The aching hearts asked and asked the bewildered minds and there was no answer. Just the unseen threat, the knowing that it was the ancient secret, killing again as it always had in the past. Killing, killing . . . Why must the secret always be the reason for death instead of the key to greatness for all men as it should be? Their eyes raised to the darkening sky for a sign from the great father, for the "breath" of the "master," for some hope from the beneficence of the unseen. But only the grim knowledge that every day one of them must die answered them. Their ancient Gods gave no other sign that night.

Each night, as they drove slowly southward, one grave was dug, one strong young brave, dead, was placed in the earth. Their prayer implored Eemeeshee to speak again as he had when the exodus was decided upon, but Eemeeshee did not answer. Hampered by the number of aged, wornout cars, the children, the old women, they drove slowly,

1269

keeping together for mutual aid when needed.

## CHAPTER III

### A New Home

WHEN they reached that part of the great American desert where the Humboldt sinks into the sands - that day they had no grave to dig! Gravely Lane looked at Stevens.

"Here in this desert must be our home. Here something keeps the curse of the daily death from us. Under our feet within the ancient rock some power for good still lives on. If we pass on, the deaths will begin again. For the evil ray people are single-minded; once set upon a course such as our deaths they don't stop until we are all dead. You know that. Upon the other side of this invisible influence, they will follow and kill us again."

"You may be right. It is hard to understand. They are not like men; the people of the underworld. They are not civilized like ourselves. It is hard to understand their slaying and cruelty, their dogged persistence in such cursing of surface men with death. But we know it is so."

A leaning sign post pointed off along a little used desert trail. "YUKA" said the sign, noncommittally. But there were scribbled Indian writings under the word, writings that only an Indian could read.

The forty cars that were left of the fifty that had started turned off the concrete into the dusty road. The wind blew hotly, lonesomely, across the wide, yellow waste. Mournfully the stolid faces looked at each other, knowing how the other's heart was hurting at this turning to the desert from their loved homes.

They had sold the cars that had broken down, and those of their dead they did not need and put the money into the common pool. Lane knew their only hope was to face their troubles with complete unity.

THAT night they sat within the lodge of Secumne in his desert fastness. There were now but twenty-five young

## THE HIDDEN WORLD

men, and some dozen aged men. Some of them were veterans, but they knew better than to go to the military with their tale. For all of them knew no white man understood the ancient secret - not to openly admit it anyway. They thought all white men cowards never to discuss the ancient secret. (But in truth white men have been carefully taught that "voices are insanity"; never to believe such silly tales. And that is hard to understand when one has been raised to respect and fear the ancient underworld.) The women and children were not admitted to the council.

Yuka had once been quite a large mining camp. Then it had been called Crockett, after the famous Indian fighter. After its brief hey-day it had been a ghost town for a long time. Now it was 'Yuka," a new name for its score of falling down frame shacks.

Secumne had taken the biggest shack. It had once been a bar-room. Now it was hung with Indian blankets, an open fire burned, weapons hung on the walls and the pelts of game. Secumne sat on a chair draped with a sheep pelt across the back.

A dozen leading men of the tribe squatted behind Secumne. Old wrinkled ones, younger eagle-eyed sturdy ones. Stevens and Lane squatted directly in front of the old chief. Behind, filling the shack, squatted or stood the twenty-five young men who survived.

Stevens smoked the long pipe, passed it to Lane. When the pipe had finally returned to Secumne, he took it in one thin hand, puffed it contentedly. There was plenty of time.

Lane handed Secumne the little paper on which John Ahahne had scribbled the pictograph message. The old man looked at it briefly, frowned, nodded, returned it. To make sure Secumne understood, Lane interpreted the message at length.

"The message is what started us away from Butte. Chance has brought us to you. Can you help us; tell us of your knowledge of the secret. What we must know to find a place that is safe for us? Your trail signs told us you would aid men of the Red Legion."

The old man looked very stupid. He looked at them a long

time. Finally the wrinkled, toothless old mouth began to talk.

"What you should know takes much telling. Not many you could find would have any information for your company. The Gods have brought you to me." The old man spoke good English. He must have been in an Indian school, long ago when young.

The company of men from Butte waited. To an outsider they looked like deeply tanned white men, in white men's clothes. But inside those clothes and that lean, rangy flesh, inside those tall silent young Americans burned the ancient fire that made the red man the feared warrior that he was. On those faces that savage courage and hardihood of the Indian sat, at home. They waited. The old one would take his time. The voice finally went on.

"You have prayed to Eemeeshee, the Breath-Master. He has answered you. I know that is true, for you have told me, and I can see you are not all liars. It has not happened for many years that Eemeeshee talked with his children. It seems that the ancient one has wakened, then. So I have much to tell you. If it had not been that you told me of your invocation to Eemeeshee - I would have little to say to you. But that is good, that Eemeeshee still answers his chosen. Now I must tell you what Eemeeshee is, and you must listen and understand me and believe. Even these who have known me many years, my own people, many of them would not believe what I am going to say. But if you wish to save yourselves from the fate that has dogged you here, you must believe me."

The old man stopped, looked at them, sounding them for unbelief, for scorn of his words. Finding only an attention and respect in their faces, he went on.

"You see, Eemeeshee is a man. He is many hundred years old. His father was still older when he died. I have been to Eemeeshee's lodge, deep under earth. I have seen him."

"YOU have seen our ancient God?" Lane rose to his feet, excitement not letting him sit still.

1272

"He exists in truth? Then all our fathers' teachings are not lies, as the white men tell us?"

"The white men are overwise sometimes. They 'know everything' because some teacher who 'knows everything' told them so, because they read a book that told them what was true and what was false. They believe they know many things they do not know. The white men are sometimes very foolish in their wisdom. Eemeeshee is not what they think. But he is not what the Red Man thinks, either. He is not a spirit! He is very different from anything you can imagine."

"How, different?" Stevens had leaned forward, watching Secumne's old face for every change of expression. It was important that they be not misled by any old dodderer. Their future depended on what they did next. Perhaps on what the old man might tell them depended the continuation or cessation of the daily deaths among their company. Perhaps the whole fate of the Red Legion, of thousands of Indians spread over half the continent - the whole Red Legion - depended on this old man's words. Stevens, too, knew there was a mighty thing to learn about such manifestations. This old one had seen him. That was important.

The old man went on.

"He is different from men, but yet only a man. In some ways he is perhaps much less than a man."

About the old chief some forty intent faces pressed closer, anxious not to miss one quavering word. Truth was in the old man's face, and he knew facts that few other living men knew about the great mystery of life: the Gods that men have worshipped and believed in always.

"Where he is, under earth, you have never seen. It is a world vastly different from our own world of sunshine and natural plant growth. Only many years of experience can give a man understanding of why things are as they are there. So much I will tell you will have to be taken as truth though it may not seem truth.

"Long, long ago - when there were no white men in all the American continent - the red men of the very far past found the ancient caverns of an Elder race. There in the caverns whole tribes lived and died and fought - and learned

1273

## THE HIDDEN WORLD

a magic never known by surface people. The Indian medicine man of those days was one who had gone to those underworld red men and learned magic - and returned to his people to teach. They learned there how to work for the unseen red men - and the remnants of their teachings, surviving in your ignorant modern minds, have brought you to this pass; have somehow brought you to me. I am the last of that kind of medicine man. There are no others that I know of. I am older than you think. For I lived a long time underground. And when I came out I found my friends had aged much more than myself. The custom of those days - of red men underground helping and teaching surface red men - has survived, even though so much time and disaster and miles of rock lie between the brothers. To you Eemeeshee is a god, only a legendary figure of the dark and ignorant past. If he is in existence, you think he is mysterious, powerful, unknowable; a kind of super ghost."

The old man paused, smiled condescendingly as upon foolish children. His smile was very sweet, he was an old, a good man, it said. One whom time had taught that only goodness and kindness are wisdom. His voice went on, a kind of mildly savage chant in the half-dark.

"But to me, who have seen him, talked to the ancient one, lived with him and served him, he is a timid thing, a misunderstood character, a vast mountain of useless and undying flesh."

The faces of the grim young men who had fled mysterious death that cut them down day by day - drew back at these words, puzzled, disappointed. They knew not what to say. Their breath sounded like a sigh in unison as the tension let up. But old Secumne went on, unnoticing, his eyes musing on things they could not know.

"EEMEESHEE is timid, as a long-necked clam is timid, as a prairie dog is timid, as a turtle is timid.

"Eemeeshee has a shell. He pokes out his head. If everything is not the way the mind of him would like it, he pulls his head in, and a year goes by before he looks again. The last time - half a century went by, so I have heard. But

1274

## THE HIDDEN WORLD

it was not that long. I am not that old. And I know him. Perhaps he has poked his head out every year.

"Eemeeshee's forefathers have lived in such shells until it is as necessary physically to him as is the actual turtle's shell. Eemeeshee never comes out of his shell. His people have lived in such machines always. Eemeeshee belongs to a very ancient family who have always lived as he is doing. It is his way – and that way is not as we know men's ways. To us, Eemeeshee is not a man. He can not live without his shell, that is a machine."

Lane stirred, rose from his haunches.

"That is very strange talk, Secumne. To some, what you say would not make sense. But we know something of what you speak. We know a few facts about the underworld. We would know more of this 'shell' of Eemeeshee's. Has Eemeeshee power? Can we go to him, as you have gone in the past? Will he teach us, help us to fight for the Red Legion? Will he show us how to work for the rights of the red men to life and a place to live? Will he help to make us strong again? These are the things we would know."

"I would tell you all these things. But it takes time, and words are very poor things with which to speak of things that the makers of the words did not know. It would be better if I took you straight to Eemeeshee myself. Then you would learn the answers to your questions and know the answers were true. I would not encourage you too much. But you are modern men. Things about Eemeeshee and his shell and about the wonders of the underworld may provide your minds with tools that to me would be useless. I am not a modern."

"You will take us to him, then?"

"Yes, my friends, I understand what you want. If it is not there where Eemeeshee still lives within his shell – it is nowhere!"

For a long time the group sat, staring into the flickering embers, waiting for the old man to talk. Now and then he would go on, then lapse into silence again.

"Eemeeshee has sat within a weird machine which he nor his fathers ever understood – and has not moved. The machine has fed him, protected him from all harm. It is that kind of machine. And all that time he has sat in possession of that fearful power which he has only occasionally used, according to legend. All that time the red men of earth were driven across the continent, have nearly vanished from earth. And Eemeeshee sat on, lazily paying no attention while his worshipping people died and vanished. He does not really think! But when we pray, sometimes Eemeeshee's (the machine's) long ears are out, and he hears the prayers of his red children. It is like the white man's radio; it hears across vast distances. But it hears only thoughts. And he cocks up these ears, sometimes, and then when he understands, he answers. Not because he wants to understand, but because the mechanism of the machine makes the heard thought so strong that his own weak thought must obey. So we answer ourselves when we know how by making Eemeeshee hear us. Then, if it makes him work for five minutes, he is tired. He shuts off the machine; he is through. He may not turn the power into the magic ears for days, months or years. For he is not a thinker, this 'God' of ours. Those mighty things he could have done for the red men, he has not done, for he had no wish to do anything."

"WHY is he like that?" Lane's eyes were filled with the mysterious meaning of the old man's words, for Lane knew enough to know it could be so, exactly as Secumne said!

"Because Eemeeshee is a dreamer. A maker of his own dreams, and a dreamer of other's dreams, too. That machine in which he has lived so long no man knows when he entered - that machine can make dreams for the worm within it. It can also make those dreams one thinks one would like to dream - make them into vivid intricate and perfect patterns of life. Eemeeshee cannot read or write, has no knowledge of life. He has never worked, never moved a muscle except to please himself with the intricate pleasures of the living machine. He is not a man. He is a feeble creature of pleasure - a great bag of almost immortal flesh that lacks all interest in life as we live it. We are just the overhead scenery with him, which he can look at or not - as he pleases."

Stevens gave a long whistle.

"That is a revelation, Secumne. These new white ray from Europe who have conquered the cavern under Butte - are they like Eemeeshee? The white ray people of the east who have left the Indians in possession of their own caverns in the west - were they like Eemeeshee before they died at the European hands?"

"I cannot say these things for certain that you ask, O Son of Courage. I can say what I have heard whispered by the voices in the night. But you know how the voices lie to us; pretend to be spirits; pretend that everything they know is a secret and that only lies can be told us of the surface. You know how mad the voices are. Yet there are voices that are not mad - that are like your John Ahahne - good and smart men of the underearth."

"Go on. What have the voices said?"

"The voices sometimes say that this white newcomer ray people who have conquered the red man's last caverns are not from Europe, but from space; from another world where things are very different. That they killed all the old friends of the people on Earth's surface; all the long lived beings like Eemeeshee within their life-machines; and that now surface man has no real friends any more under the rocks of earth. Only corsairs from space, who seek only to keep men ignorant and weak. But I do not believe it, for the voices seem so often to be like European voices: men who have learned English well, but are yet Europeans; Continentals. But all the voices agree that the leaders of these rays, everywhere, are too often mad. The people who have control rays are mad, do not think at all of anything but their own pleasure, can not even think effectively of precautions for their own safety."

"There are many such as Eemeeshee left, do you think?"

"No, my friend. I think that even Eemeeshee is alive only by accident. I think that most of his kind, his feeble, peculiar race of men-within-a-machine-shell has been nearly killed off by the newcomers in the caverns."

"These newcomers could well be from the surface, who

1277

have introduced modern gangster methods into the strange cavern world."*

"No, the reports of them are too peculiar. They contend they do not think as men. Or do not think at all. Just pleasure and cruelty."

"Lazy, like Eemeeshee, but in a different way, eh?"

"That is right. Now, if you don't mind - since we are starting in the morning for the place I spoke of, and I am an old man - I must go to bed. All your questions will be much better answered by the actuality than by my words. Once down there you will learn these things."

"I suppose you are right. I would rather see this immortal Eemeeshee than to hear about him - if he is as harmless as you say."

"He is not exactly harmless. But he has no will to slay anyone in particular; no reason to harm you. Eemeeshee can fight quite well or he would not be alive."

"Well however it may be - goodnight."

## CHAPTER IV

### The Finding of Eemeeshee

ALL the next day six cars drove across the desert. There was little or no visible trail but they were following an ancient forgotten road, and the cars found it not too difficult. Old Secumne, toward the close of the day, indicated a stopping place. The cars drew up in a line, facing the wall of a canyon. There was no particular reason for stopping that Lane could see.

Darkness was on them when the evening meal was finished. Secumne rose from the fire, walked to the canyon wall. From his blanket roll he had taken a little flute. Now he blew three notes upon the flute. A high one, a low one, and one soft in between in pitch.

---

*It is a peculiarity of the caves that there is a weird mixture of ancient and modern. Imitation of ancient dress is amazingly authentic. - Ed.

1278

## THE HIDDEN WORLD

A vast muffled rumble answered from within the wall of rough rock. Slowly a great section tipped, swiveling slowly outward, pivoting on its center. Exposed on both sides of the balanced section of rock was a tunnel, wide enough, big enough for four motor cars abreast. Two cars could have driven in on each side of the pivoted rock. The tunnel led down as far as their lights reached. Lane stood, overcome by the magnitude of this proof of the old Indian's words. Hearing of such things was one thing, seeing them quite another.

"Who built such a thing?"

"It is the work of the ancient ones who built all through the under-rock of earth. No one knows words to describe or name them today. But presently I will show you wall pictures of their tremendous beauty and strength. They were giant men. There are few such doors left any more. This one has been protected from erosion by circumstances. Too, in times not too long past, our own forefathers, the red men who served such as Eemeeshee, chipped away the stone, kept the door open, protected and cared for it. Unless such care goes on the door will be lost forever. Such has happened to many doors into the underworld. One by one they disappear forever. But of late years, the voices tell me there are many new openings being made."

"It doesn't seem possible that time would leave such a thing intact to operate."

"Men have spent much time and labor upon it. See how earthen bulwarks have been built to keep the water from flowing here. How the rocks that might fall and block it have been cleared away above. Once there were many hands to serve the fathers of Eemeeshee, and Eemeeshee, if he had had the mind to use them. But such as he have little mind to use people."

Old Secumne's voice was filled with a strange weariness, as though the contemplation of the facts about such creatures as the Indian God Eemeeshee was very painful to him.

As the cars trundled into the smooth roadway, picked up speed, Lane asked Secumne:

"How is it that Eemeeshee has survived the death you

1279

think has caught up with his like in other places?"

"He is not easy to kill. Too, he is not feared, for he is peculiar, timid. They are used to having such as him about. It is not wise to try to kill such as the old one without necessity. They sometimes know mighty things, which they do not use until someone arouses them from their dreams."

"Finding that the legendary Gods have had a real existence, and that something that was once worshipped as a God still lives on when all belief in such existence has disappeared, is a disappointment. I suppose all Gods everywhere in the centuries past have been just such creatures."

"They have not all been like Eemeeshee, no! But many have. Others, I learned long ago, do not exist, but are imitated by people in the caverns for no reason but custom and mischievousness. But to tell men anything about such subjects I have always found nearly impossible. It is good to find that the Red Legion itself is not a legend, but a reality. It is good to know that the Legion has many members, knows enough to realize that the old tales had a truth about them, a mighty truth."

THE cars wound down and down. Driving was no task, the road was broad, straight and level except for a gradual and hardly noticeable curve, and level as new laid concrete. Here and there slight shifts of the rock strata had raised bumps, sudden steps, where a drop or a raise had taken place, but usually these were easily negotiable as the unevenness had been filled at some time in the past with rubble.

As the way led deeper and deeper into the earth, these shiftings of the rock grew less and less. At last they disappeared altogether.

"How far to the old one?" Stevens leaned toward Secumne, sitting in the back seat with Lane. His dark, aquiline face was intent, curious.

"Couple hours yet. Can't drive fast, can't tell. Maybe rock fall, maybe barricades put up since. Haven't been here for twenty years now."

Lane spoke to Stevens.

# THE HIDDEN WORLD

"Just what do we expect to get out of him, anyway. Hadn't we better discuss what we are going to say to him, and then let Secumne do the talking? He knows the ancient rigamaroles by which such beings are propitiated. It isn't as if we were going to discuss a point of law with a judge on the bench, you know. We don't really have much idea what we're trying to do."

Stevens looked at Secumne.

"When we get there, you try and arouse some feeling in the old one for the red man and his struggle to remain - to grow great again in his own way. Tell how the white man has displaced us while our guardian, Eemeeshee has dreamed away the life that should have been devoted to preserving the Indian and his way of life, his racial culture and attainments. Tell him that now is his last chance to be what his children have always thought him to be. Try and arouse some spark in his heedless heart. Then, if you see life in his brain and a regard for the red man, tell him we belong to a legion - the last organized red men on the continent. That we will bring members of the legion here to learn from him the way of the Elder Gods. That he must only teach. That if there is fighting to be done, we will do it for him. There is no need for him to disturb his peace or come out of his dreams. After he has taught one of us we will guard him and serve him while we teach the others ourselves. Understand?"

"I catch. I'll tell him what he should have been told a hundred years ago - a hundred and fifty - or what his father should have known three hundred years ago."

The cars were now passing the gray dust-shrouded shapes of the wonder work of the Elder race, but old Secumne gave no sign of calling a halt. Steven's eyes darted right and left, watching the dust-covered mystery that was the machinery of a science now lost from earth. A tremendous emotion was aroused in him as he realized what there was here for his people that had been denied them by the ignorance of such as Eemeeshee, and of such as Secumne. He turned to the old man.

"Why have you never brought any of the educated young

men of your tribe here? Why have you hidden this knowledge of yours for your people?"

"When I was younger," answered the old man sadly, "I tried to do those things you have in mind. The young men laughed at me! I tried very hard, brought some men here to show them. All went well till they saw the body and terrible appearance of Eemeeshee. Then they laughed, or swore, or fled. They could not think right of the ancient one and he grew angry, slew some, chased the others away. They had not the vision or courage. I have waited all my life for seekers such as you. Now you have come. I warn you, Eemeeshee knows your thought. Try and think correctly, or your efforts will end in failure. Eemeeshee is not such a man as you and I. His heredity is very different."

"You mean to say you brought educated young Indians here and they took no advantage of what there is here to be learned - to be used for our race? Explain!"

"Some few of them did learn what it all meant. They tried to lead others, to teach as you plan. But they failed to convince others, became at last discouraged and bitter as I have become. Men are very foolish. They cannot believe in anything that is greater than their school books. Sometimes I think it were better had they never gone to school! It closed their minds to all greater truths. They have refused me.

"They have refused the wisdom of the underworld and of the past because their teachers did not tell them of it in their school books. So they knew it could not be. I got tired of being laughed at. I took my women and my children and moved here to this place where you have found me. I am very tired of life."

Stevens nodded grimly.

"I think we may find a remedy for your difficulties. Some men told me of you when I was quite young. They did not laugh. You have been laughed at in public; but those who did not laugh have believed you without talking about it very much. Now we have it again: a door to the ancient secret. We knew this thing was true, but the entrances were closed

1282

to us. We did not know how to lay our hands on the ancient mech. We did not know an open entrance.

THE tall, white figure in the roadway waved them to a halt. He was white as a fish's belly, but his features were purest Indian, with a great hawk nose, wide nostrils, high cheekbones - and a lean, starved, greyhound body. His limbs were bone thin under the long white ceremonial robe. He was very old, but somehow vigorous. His words were purest Quemaya, and only Secumne understood the almost extinct tongue well.

"Welcome to the ancient realm of the Breath-Master. It has been long since pilgrims have found their way to their God. Give me your names that I may acquaint the mighty one with your presence and learn if he will grant you sight of his glory."

Secumne answered gravely in the same tongue.

"We are Pilgrims come bearing news and asking for the aid of the great one. We have much to give, and we may receive much. Our news is for the ears of the great one only. He may remember my name: I was a servant here in the days, long ago, of my youth. I am Secumne. He may also know that Eemeeshee is a real being. They are Jack Stevens and Eonee Lane. They represent a great legion of red men, the last of our once mighty race who still preserve courage to plan for the future of the Indian. It will be a mighty pleasure to Eemeeshee to know that his red sons still need him, still want his leadership and his wisdom. Tell the Breath-Master that if our fathers had sought and found the way to his home that we would not now need his help. For he would not have turned his face away from his red·sons. Tell him, too, we bring him news of danger to his life from other beings who have come to the caverns of the Gods of the past. They will kill him, if he does not know they come, does not cease his mighty dreaming and look at the world at his feet."

The tall, white-robed, skeleton-thin Indian turned and walked away through a vast doorway in the boring that was the road. The eight men got out of the cars; built a fire; began to prepare a meal. Little was said. There was too much

1283

to say for words to do their duty.

Lane sat by the fire, waiting for the women to complete the cooking. He heard a faint scuffing behind. He turned slowly, and a cold fear of the unknown struck into him.

Gazing at him not three feet away was a face. A face belonging to a great white spider! Twenty feet those thin white limbs extended, that little round body poised upon the fragility, looking at him with a human face. The huge black eyes, hanging long hair, the straggly pale beard of ivory yellow, the body which was like a man's if a man had been stretched magically across a twenty-foot span and left to live on that way. Lane could only stare and lick his dry lips. He could not speak.

The long, so much too long, thin arm reached out, touched Lane's cheek cautiously, almost caressingly. The fingers, three times a normal man's finger length and three times a man's fingers in thinness, in fragility, felt slowly, carefully over his face, touched his hair, his shirt, his hand. Satisfied, the towering, thin height eased slowly to a squatting position.

Then, the great round eyes watching Lane, the long arm reached out fifteen feet away, dipped quickly into the cooking pot, snared a bit of boiled meat out of the hot liquid, burned its fingers. The mouth opened to a round pink O, then let out a shrill yip like a hurt puppy.

The incongruous life sat there, unnoticed by the others, sucking its long fingers and eyeing Lane speculatively. Lane spoke.

"You speak English? Who are you?"

The wide, too round eyes looked puzzled at Lane, clicked its tongue. "Tch tch." But it did not answer.

"Secumne! Come here!" Lane did not call loudly, his voice might startle the strange visitor.

THE old man rose from his place by the farther fire, came slowly through the dark. He stood, his stolid, lined old face looking at the visitor.

"Tch tch," said Secumne.

"Tch thcheeee. Chee tch tcch. Tch."

# THE HIDDEN WORLD

"What do you have to say about this?" Lane asked.

"This is one of the lost of the caves. His people did not use the ancient rays to stay healthy, the conditions of the dark caverns have made his race, bit by bit, year by year and century by slow century, into what you see. He is to a man what a potato sprout in a dark cellar is to a potato plant in the hot sun. He is what is called a 'creep, a spider man.' He is not stupid, but he does not speak any real language. The tongue has no more than a hundred meanings. 'Food, water, sleep, wakewell, ill'; such sounds are all you need to learn to talk to 'Tch Tch'."

Lane did not answer. He only looked at Tch Tch. So the ever-dark had made this out of man?

Far off, down in the dim cavern road, Lane could see other tall white spider shapes, standing still - or moving swiftly on their incredible stick-like limbs. It was hard to realize that their parents had been men like himself, some centuries before. Hard to realize how very greatly it is true that environment determines the organism and its shape and nature so definitely, so absolutely.

The soft old voice of Secumne murmured:

"This one, Tch Tch, is the leader. The leader is always named Tch Tch. Mostly they do not have names. They are really but a kind of intelligent animal entirely indigenous to the caverns."

Lane turned to Secumne a face on which was written the beginning of that awe that was going to claim him utterly before he had learned but a minute part of what the caves could teach. That awe of the infinite nature of energy and her products that is to surface man hidden by the everyday humdrum activity, by the limited number of the works of nature that modern man observes. The terrific majesty of the cavern works, built by the hands of a race so superior as to be not really men at all, but Gods, would dispel for-even the limiting bonds his puny life-experience had placed upon Lane's mind. It is a potent alchemy for a healthy mind; the revelations the caverns have to offer.

Even as Lane turned to gaze again into the fire and try to guiet his throbbing thought into sanity in spite of the mighty truths his deduction was presenting to his trained, logical mind; even as he composed himself and strove to pull his mind back from the gulfs which it was leaping, from the gorging of its hunger upon the mighty meaning circumstance had laid before it . . .

. . . a soft shuffle of sandaled feet behind him brought with their sound an alien perfume, a rustle and a sensing that is to virile man irresistible, that which that black magic of Mother Earth's ancient devising sends the blood leaping through the body shouting, "woman, woman!"

Lane whirled, crouched on his heels as he was, to see moving toward him from the dark the white, unmistakable form of a woman of normal size and remarkable appearance. She was not dressed in the long funereal garments which the skeleton-thin servitor of Eemeeshee had worn. Instead a brief fringed and beaded loincloth was her sole attire - except for a collar of rich Indian bead work resting upon her shoulders. So must have looked the women of his ancestral line, centuries ago before the white man came, as they moved to the marriage rites clothed in beauty and courage and becoming feminine humility and finding it covering enough.

THE pale face with its too large black eyes came closer to Lane, and one by one the men looked up at her and stared, their eyes fixed upon her as by magnetism polarized. Lane rose, and the blood leaped through him. The woman smiled. An eerie something gripped Lane. He bowed on one knee, something that he had never done. Her voice came to him then, a sultry, smiling voice, full of little undertones and an understanding of men.

"You are the one named Eonee Lane. The Master has sent me to bring you and the one named Stevens to him. The Master is greatly interested that you should find your way to him still - when the men of the surface have forgotten him for so long."

"We are very interested, too. And who do we have the honor of addressing?"

"My name is Saba. I am called the Keeper of the

# THE HIDDEN WORLD

Women. I am very glad you have come." There was an accompaniment of subtle meaning to her remark that Lane was not sure he heard or imagined. It was quite possible that she was glad to meet men from the surface if the thin robed skeleton who had met them first was a criterion of the men of the caverns. Or if "Tch Tch" was a sample of the manhood hereabout.

She turned and led off into the dark, and Lane and Stevens followed her. The women of the party turned their dark eyes upon the departing form of Saba wistfully. She was so much a woman it was hard to have one's man send his eyes after her realizing that themselves were so much less than Saba.

Lane and Stevens followed the supple silhouette through the half dark.

"Into the mysterious 'shell' of the ancient god - the 'Breath-Master'," thought Lane. "Now we will see what the 'mighty power' so many of my ancestors have worshipped really is."

Down a long winding ramp Saba led them, never looking back, her ears telling her of their movement. A light glow lamp in her hand was the only light. Apparently Saba carried it for their benefit, for she did not appear to look at her surroundings, seemed to know her way in the utter darkness, seemed to move, like a bat, by the echo of the sounds from the surroundings. Lane and Stevens followed the tiny glow in her hand, trusted to luck and to Saba that all was well.

Quite abruptly they were no longer in a dark cavern, but had entered the titanic, brightly-lit luxury that is the God's home, when it has been left intact. This place had been treated kindly by Time, or had been carefully preserved by endless work by many hands through the centuries.

The walls were of crystal, a crystal that was cut with gigantic incut line-carvings, like Swedish cut-glass. Terrific figures of the unequalled giant physique of the Elder race moved across the transparent planes of the walls in the breathtaking splendor of form that is the Elder art work alone. The great couches of spring metal were thrown across with gleaming silk of blue, worked in gold, while a swinging incense burner exhaled a softening haze into the air, a haze

1287

that was a too-exotic scent of the Elder race's stores.

In the midst of this vaulting fabric of stone and shining crystal and carved alien figures and hazy air and utterly lonely luxury sat Eemeeshee, an Eemeeshee who was surrounded by a tremendous machine built of crystalline plastic and gleaming, glittering polished metals; or fluid flowing colorfully through coils and tubes beneath his feet; of glowing dials and leaping energies within vast cylinders before his eyes: of many great cubical screen cavities wherein the whole upper world might be brought to focus. This machine in which lay the great fat body of the motionless Eemeeshee was the work of a Master of the ancient machine art which has never been on Earth since the Golden Age.

EEMEESHEE turned his vast, horrible head slowly upon them as Saba's sandaled feet sluffed on the smooth plastic of the floor. Within Lane's breast a terrific fear of the unknown, an overwhelming repulsion struggled to send him screaming and shuddering back into the darkness outside the alien luxury of this roost of terror. For Eemeeshee was truly no longer a man, if ever his race had been man. His flesh lay within the crystal complexities of the machine as though it were an ugly dough kneaded by some alchemist into a shape to frighten off the devil, and left there by his own fearful hands refusing the work. A great white sluggish pulsing thing, surmounted by two vast pillars that were his arms stretched out along the dial and switch banks of the mechanism that was his immortal home. And the face that he turned on them as his sausage-like, two-foot-long fingers ceased their slow spidering glide along the instrument panel - that face that surrounded those eyes was itself enough to give a weak man instant madness. But the terror of the eyes was the thing that held Lane and Stevens motionless though every instinct shouted "flee." Those eyes that surmounted that vast twist of white flesh and had watched the world for unknown centuries, held all the weariness and boredom; all the melancholy and hopelessness; all the alien, cold unhuman thought that is not thought as we know it. All the things that man does not believe in, were in those eyes. A lonely, terrible ugliness of spirit sat in that face. An ugliness of spirit that is the lack of identity, of brotherhood, with any other living thing. Lane read in the terrible face with its foot-long nose hooked and sickeling upward over the chin, that this being had never realized there was a kinship between him and any living thing. He was an alien entity, whatever his antecedents may have been. Eemeeshee did not speak, he only looked incuriously upon the two young Indian men, and his eyes inspected them as one inspects a fly upon a window pane with the utmost disinterest and careless acknowledgement that the fly has life. The ego that is man's normal possession shrank within Lane, and a vast sensing of cold aloneness came to him from Eemeeshee.

Saba raised her voice in a long sing-song of gibberish. It was an ancient language, a parent to the Quemaya, but not one that was understandable to either of them. These awful eyes rested for a brief moment on Saba, and Saba nodded and was gone.

They were alone with the terrible regard of those alien, inhuman eyes. They knew that he could read their thoughts of him with the mech with which his fingers slowly toyed. They knew that their thoughts of him were not complimentary, but how can a man think differently of what he sees than he does think? Lane knew this thing was getting off on the wrong foot, some way, but the key to making of this meeting with Eemeeshee anything but a terror was beyond him.

At last, when the long silence and slow regard of the eyes was becoming unbearable, a ray laced softly down upon them from the touch of his sausage-long finger upon a dial, and a soft flood of thought swept into them from Eemeeshee. A vast understanding of this being flooded Lane at this touch of the mind upon his own. The thought queried softly, almost timidly, "Who and what are you? What do you want of Eemeeshee?"

Lane's spirits rose now. Mentally he resolved to make a real effort at being understood. Carefully he began at the beginning of their trouble in Butte; of the Red Legion and what it meant; of what they had been taught by the old men of their tribe about Eemeeshee; of how Indians had always prayed to Eemeeshee and had been rewarded with oblivion and a futility of nonentity for their worship. All these thoughts of themselves and what they hoped Eemeeshee might do for them mingled swiftly into a vast message to that atrophied might.

LANE knew he was making an impression, for a pale pink flush suffused that colorless great moon of horribly flattened flesh that was a face, the great nostrils opened a little, the lonely, world-weary eyes lit up with interest and again the meaning flowed into him from Eemeeshee.

"What is this people's power who have driven you forth, and why do you think they're a threat to me?"

Lane leaped upon his opportunity.

"Eemeeshee, these alien ray people come from afar, they have killed all the machine dwellers wherever their rays have touched. There is no reason to think they will not kill you too, when they know where you are and why they have not known of you before."

"Who told you they killed the race of the machine dwellers? Who told you these people killed the Gods of the caves?"

"Has someone told you they did not kill? They have killed many of the Red Legion with no cause. Why should they not try to kill you?"

"I have become tired of life. It might be interesting if someone tried to kill me. Tell me more of these people."

Lane told the great emotionless being all that he knew of the newcomers to the northern caverns. Softly, mildly, the great face listened, the great lazy mind turned the thoughts idly and visibly before Lane's mental listening.

How to rouse the time-atrophied soul of that great body? How to give him human anger and human will to survive and create? Lane's mind leaped and struggled and wrestled with the problem. This great, flat, twisted, lazy whiteness of flesh seemed to Lane to typify, to be the whole race of men who do not think or try to solve life's problems, all the deadwood of the race of man rolled into one great spirit and put there to dwell forever in a terrible enigmatic punishment of one soul for all the sins of omission of all men. How to rouse such a devil of living nothingness into a Godlike fury of will toward creation and striving toward a greater, fuller life for all men?

How to fecundate that great thing with the red flame of courage that burned, Lane knew, in the men of the Red Legion? How to make him desire to forward the real purpose of life, to fight for them and their goals understandingly and eagerly?

"Let me show you my men? Looking into their minds, see their love for their children, for the great legends of the red men of the past, see their spirit seeking a method to make a way of life for the red man that will lead again to greatness as it was before such as you turned their faces from the red man and fell a-dreaming here within your God-built machines. Think what your duty toward your fellow men may be. Think, Eemeeshee! These men would fight to the death for you! Will you lie down and die like a coward before the coming of the evil thing that has killed their brothers? Are you a coward, Eemeeshee?"

Eemeeshee slowly turned the words within his mind. His hand idly turned the dials, and within the great cubical screens Lane could see the small encampment of his men where their fire burned beside the great cavern road.

Slowly, one by one, Eemeeshee sent his seeking telaug beam into each mind, read there all the thoughts, looked idly at Lane to note that he was watched as he did what Lane suggested.

And even as Lane dared to hope that the life in that mind might take fire from the desperation of his followers; even as Lane dared to send his mind along the vision of what the future might be with all the wisdom of this terrific being to guide them . . . the enemy struck again!

A terrible ray lanced, searing and deadly, down into that luxurious, lonely nest of crystal and blue and gold in that chamber. Struck, burning and smashing at the vast white coils and ugly billows of soft flesh, of ancient, pink-and-white life, struck rending at that soft vastness of Eemeeshee

1291

in a frenzied effort to bring death quickly before retaliation.

Lane fell to the floor, blinded and burnt from the ray flashing past his head, and a terrible odor of death, of burning flesh filled the great quiet room that had seen so much time go quietly by - and now this had come to Eemeeshee.

## CHAPTER V

### Saba

SABA was looking out upon the new-comers. Knowingly, thoughtfully her fertile, infinitely educated mind, revolved the new thing - men - in her life. Since a little girl she had spent all her waking hours seeing that the needs and wishes of the great Eemeeshee were filled. All the sensuous desires of his wholly mental life she had minded, too, making with her fertile mind all the images he might desire to watch augmented and developed into life fullness in the solidographic dream mech.

All those antique records she had read had given her avid young mind a food that has not been properly given to man since the Gods left the earth. She was vastly more than mortal; she was what simpler people call a white fairy, a sorceress. She knew mighty things that could be done with simple materials, she knew vast secrets of energy and life and matter without really realizing that she was superior to man. For all her time she was taken up ministering to the greedy laziness that was the mind of Eemeeshee. She had little time to think of other things in her life except Eemeeshee and his needs.

Now, suddenly, into her life of even tenor, of fixed and, to her, perfect habits, had come a turmoil of new factors. The ways of her life, the wishes of her soul, had that night turned into a new heated channel. The tall, strong, and grim-faced man, Lane, had made an impression on her vital inner self; a self that had not faced man in all reality, ever before. Only sometimes over the rays had she looked upon men far overhead - and mostly their thoughts were too simple and unbeautiful to interest her.

Saba knew, now, that no more would she content herself with knowing men from afar over the rays. She realized that from the fire of striving within the mind of the tall grim strangers, fleeing before a mysterior death, from the mind of Eonee Lane, their leader, and within the mind of the sleeker, stronger Stevens, that she would no more be content with the lazy empty life and luxury of pandering to the great appetite that ruled all this cavern. Saba was taking stock of herself for the first time in her life.

She had drifted with the calm currents of events, events that never happened here in the quiet dark, had accepted the half-life of this place too easily. Something had now been added which had transformed her selfish, lazy reflection of Eemeeshee's atrophied self-will to a sudden realization that she had been letting life go by while she too dreamed away everything that life might be in the luxury of the false sensing of what life was not of the dream mech.

About Saba where she leaned against her great old deliciously ornate vision mech in thought, watching the scene of Lane and Stevens before Eemeeshee, about her slept or dawdled some two score other women, of all ages. They were the harem which Eemeeshee kept in deference to custom among his kind, rather than for any real need or desire he had for them. There were few men in Eemeeshee's "court," for Eemeeshee usually detested men and their ambitions plaguing him to effort he did not desire to make. He banished the children of the place, if they were men, before they came of an age to make trouble. The old priest Watusojhe served as his advisor and general factotum. A half-dozen youths, children of the women, supposed to be children of Eemeeshee, but in truth fathered by the wanderers of the caverns - those men who spend their lives searching the endless labyrinths of the dark for the treasures that they sell to the space ships that come sometimes to certain customary places for this purpose. (The age-old custom of secrecy of the caverns forbids trade with surface men. Too, men of the surface world have little to offer that cavern people recognize as value. The rich, tremendous value of the

1293

ancient profuseness of productions of the vastly superior race make the poor values of surface man of little account.)

But Eemeeshee's solitary ways had given these women of his a hunger for human kind, and the strong youth and complex thought of these newcome Indians of modern surface educated ways was to them a wonderful thing. So it was that Saba and several others were watching the encampment and the scene within the crystal chamber over the ray mech, while the guard ways - which of old custom were supposed to be watched by someone always and which reached for many miles to the four quarters of direction - were now perfunctorily watched from a distance. On the screens, if they had looked, could have been seen the great rolling ray weapons in their ray-armored tanks sweeping nearer and nearer from the north.

But Saba was not thinking of attack, for there had been no attack in her lifetime.

Nor, in all Eemeeshee's centuries-old memory, had she noted in her reading of his mind any attack of importance for so many, many years. When the blazing bolts of energy flung themselves into Eemeeshee's crystal nest, there was little they knew to do about it. Warfare was the thing farthest from their minds as well as from Eemeeshee's thought.

EVEN so, Saba had talked with the wandering treasure hunters, and knew a great deal about warfare by hearsay. In anticipation of such attack she had occasionally practiced with the great weapon beams that sat in ordered ranks everywhere about the great ancient dwelling place. And as she saw the searing bolts of deadly dis-fire come seeking them out over the long pale penetrays, she leaped to one of the tremendous weapons and sent the vast vision beam flying along the enemy ray paths for their source.

Horror struck into Saba, even the Saba who had experienced all the horror and terror that God brains could conceive in their synthetic adventure records. For the thought that flowed back to her along these conductive, teleaugmentive vision beams; that leaped out at her from the great vision screen: that thought was not human. Humans the men

## THE HIDDEN WORLD

looked like but what lived beneath their skulls made even Saba shudder and start back in fear and trembling.

They were things sent by a greater thing, a thing she had not met before in her limited life - and Saba had no time to analyze why these apparently normal appearing men were so luridly, so evilly different from men in their minds.

She had no time for flinching, and Saba, seeing the enemy that had followed the caravan of fleeing Indian men, that had paused as the road led into territory unknown to them, that had been feeling their way along under the great mass of rocks that was their sky closer and closer to Eemeeshee ever since they had left familiar territory, acted.

They felt for an instant that terrible nearness of death they had brought to so many in their life. Then they died very quickly.

The horror that Saba had felt when she had seen and heard their thought upon the vision screen made her sear the bodies of those human beings until there was no more horror to hear from the minds, nothing to see, only a scorched, burnt, flaming, smoking place where their ray cars had been. On the cavern road where their wheeled ray mech had drawn up in line to steady the screens for firing sight, to lay down a blanket of accurate fire, now was only many scattered bits of smoking metal.

\* \* \*

UNKNOWING why the attack had ceased as suddenly as it had begun, Lane and Stevens stood there, looking at the strange spectacle of the great soft worm-like body of the vast Eemeeshee turned into a raging, writhing, stricken creature.

Midway of the long softness had appeared a great burned hole where a ray had drilled him, and one of the long soft fleshy arms was cut nearly in two midway from the soft billows that were his shoulder. Lane could not help thinking as he watched that mayhap the rays who had struck at Eemeeshee had done him more of a service than a harm, for the lassitude that seemed a part of him had also been sheared away by the sudden hiss of the burning rays.

## THE HIDDEN WORLD

That great white thing reared upward and the unwounded arm moved with a terrible angry swiftness here and there upon the keyboard of switches; the many keys like an organ keyboard; the many pedals that protruded near his feet. He pressed, now here, now there, and on the score of cubical screens that made up the greater part of the body of the transparent machine appeared swiftly scene after scene of the great empty underworld of unending tubes of highways, of tiers of vast empty chambers filled with their dust-laden complexities of machines and forgotten wealth. Farther and farther Eemeeshee searched for the source of the attack.

Finally he found the smoking series of spots where the enemy ray mech had drawn up for attack. Wonderingly he looked at it, and as he looked the soft voice of Saba could be heard explaining to Eemeeshee that she had found and slain the attackers already.

Now Eemeeshee sagged again and the temporary vigor that had flooded him passed away. He began to moan and weep like a whipped child.

A score of Saba's women and Saba swept into the chamber, their sandaled feet making swift whispers of haste and pity, and Eemeeshee's wounds were carefully washed and treated and bound up. Lane and Stevens stood through it all, an ignored part of the great vacant immensity that is always the atmosphere of the Elder caverns.

At last Saba came forth from the transparent winding passages of the machine where Eemeeshee lay like the great pupa of some vast insect thing of the past that was presently going to hatch into a winged god but had certainly not done so yet.

Saba paused, her lithe, full woman's form holding a great golden basin of water on her hip, her arm draped with bandages, in her hand a pair of ancient scissors a foot long.

"Saba," said Lane, seeing now his chance, "this occurrence proves something to me that I wish you and Eemeeshee might fully understand. That is: you need our Red Legion terribly here. This attack will not be the last. There will be more and more such attacks, and the next will not be so easily wiped out by one pair of hands as was this one. You need our young Indian braves, trained and ready and watching from every far flung ray post. You need steadily to grow and grow and have more and more strength until there is no ray group anywhere to face your strength. Will you explain this to Eemeeshee?"

"I do not need to. Even now I saw in his angry mind just such plans. I will go ahead and have my women train your folk in the uses of the rays, and we will put your plans swiftly into operation. You call in from their far homes the rest of your Red Legion and we will make this place something different from what it has been. It will be good to have new faces, new eager spirits about. I like your plans."

LANE did not wait for more. Stevens by his side, they hastened back to the camp of the refugees and explained the situation. The attack had gone unnoticed by the camp. The Indians slept peacefully in their blankets.

The next morning the great hidden door in the rock lifted, and two of the cars that had come in went out again. In the cars were two of the young braves intent upon delivering their message to the other centers of the Red Legion. Stevens had told them to go in person to each of the headquarters of the Legion and tell them in their own words just what had happened, what Eemeeshee was, and that they were all needed to defend their ancient God and the gateway to the vast wisdom of the past.

Eemeeshee lay in his great crystal nest and glowered and growled and nursed his hurts. Saba and Lane and Stevens worked hard daily, teaching, getting a force of ready hands upon the ancient ray controls, getting prepared as swiftly as they might for a repetition of the attack from the north. Every day they spread their force a little, posting men to the four quarters with the old rays reaching out for forty miles to watch steadily, sweeping across the innumerable passages through the rock where attack might come. They were now vastly safer than before the attack, but Lane knew that anyone really conversant with the uses of the ancient mechanisms must be able to overcome them. For they knew so little of it. If it broke . . .

Only Saba and one or two of the women knew the least thing about repairing the machines. They were too green, as Saba explained, really to fight with the weapons as the old accounts told her they were meant to be fought with.

But the attack did not come, and now into the great door every night came three or four or a dozen of the men of the Red Legion; men from Oregon; men from Canada; men from the pueblos; Mexican Indians sent their number. Swiftly the word spread and steadily their numbers grew.*

Now papooses shouted and ran in the gloomy so-long-empty caverns, and cooking fires gleamed by the hundreds. Indian women swayed in their tribal mating dances, the braves sprang and whooped in the war-dance. Life had come to this place of Eemeeshee's. And over the new activity glowered ever the transformed Eemeeshee, and one could read ever in his heard thought: "Vengeance. Eemeeshee has a way to vengeance."

Said Saba:

"No more does Eemeeshee flood the chambers with the dream images and wallow in the stim-dreams of beauty and wonder. No more does he take pleasure day after day and year after year. These wounds have changed him - he has waked up! I have never seen him so intent upon anything as he is now upon growing strong and fighting with these enemies who attacked without warning. His anger burns steadily,

---

*Temples and Caves - from Enc. Brit.

. . . but in many very ancient sancturaries the place of a temple is taken by a natural or artificial grotto (Phoenician Astarte grottoes - the grotto of Cynthus in Delos), or else the temple is built over a subterranean opening (as at Delphi), and while this may . . . be connected with the cult of telluric deities . . .

The altar in front of temple had its prototype in altars at the mouths of sacred caves . . .

The influence of the cave temple . . . undeniable widespread type of sanctuary.

Certain adyta in Greece were actually subterranean and the association of oracles with caves is well known.

1298

higher and higher. He has taught me many things he formerly denied me. Come, I will show you what he taught me yesterday."

Saba took Lane to a great round machine. A mouth about three feet across in the center of the mech gave a view of successive coils reaching in, each coil a little smaller than the other to the bottom of the inward cone. She switched on the power and from the big orifice came a strong bass hum - a pulsing of power that streamed from the opening in a visible flow of power.

"What is it?" asked Lane. "It looks something like a cyclotron."

"This cyclotron you speak of; what is that?"

"It is a device they use to speed up an electric particle. There are several kinds, depending on the kind of particle they want to speed up. They bombard matter with it: it becomes more radioactive. It was used in developing the atom bomb."

"This, then," Saba smiled, "is a 'cyclotron-in-reverse.' This is used to slow down the flow of certain kinds of particles until the body can catch and hold them. It makes the energy that is always about us available to the body by slowing down the speeds at which the parts of energy travel. Each coil is creator of a magnetic field which attracts, catches and slows the flight of the bits of energy until as it emerges it is a slow flood of the stuff from which all matter is synthesized by nature - and the body of the person in the flow takes in the energy just as we take food in through the mouth. It prepares energy for the absorption by that kind of matter which our body is made of. At least, such was the explanation Eemeeshee gave me as he pointed out the uses to which I was to put this machine and others like it. It is to be used to make our warriors strong and smart and able to learn quickly what they must learn to defeat this horrible enemy who has attacked us."

LANE put out his hand, immersed it in the flow of energy from the orifice. His hand seemed to swell, to feel strong. The lassitude of relaxation went out of it - strength pulsed within his fingers and flowed up his arm. His whole body felt invigorated just from the immersion of his hand.

Saba watched him.

"Put your head in, if you want really to note the effects. It makes the brain immensely more active. And the effect continues long afterward. It is like charging a battery, a battery of life energy, with life energy."

Lane stooped, dipped his head momentarily into the pulsing flow of strange electricray. Through his mind flashed a picture of vast plans for the Red Legion, of great conquests of just such valuable secrets of the old machines of the caves, and of vast conquests and growth for the Red Legion. As he removed his head, these pictures died slowly out, but his mind remained sharper, clearer, he knew he was vastly more alive.

"Did he show you anything else?" this new and sharper Lane asked Saba, his eyes glittering now with energy and enthusiasm. This machine for invigorating his men had heartened him.

Saba led him toward another great machine, somewhat similar in appearance but with a greatly more complicated keyboard of control dials.

"Yes. He showed me this, saying: 'If you need monetary metals, you can make them with this.' It is a similar appearing machine - the same cone of great coils reaching inward, but its use is certainly vastly different. It also slows up the particles that circulate always about us, makes of them a concentrated flow; but it has atunements that regulate what kind of particle is slowed. Watch and you will see why. Have you some base metal?"

Lane searched his pockets, found only a fifty cent piece, some pennies and a nickel.

Saba took the pennies and the nickel from him and placed them on a sliding tray before the mouth of the power cone, slid the tray into the center of the orifice. She pulled the activating lever.

The hum rose and rose in pitch, and as Lane watched Saba adjusted the dial to a marking.

"See, Eonne, this marking is a symbol that means gold.

There is a mark for each element you want to produce, though these markings can only be used for materials heavier in the atomic table than the material you place in the flow."

Presently she withdrew the tray, picked up the coins and handed them to Lane. Lane looked at them, hefted them. They had increased greatly in weight, changed to a red gold in color. He took his knife, cut one of the coins. It was pure gold.

"Transmutation!" ejaculated Lane. "Here we have the means to finance an army, an empire. Eemeeshee should get angry oftener; God know what we might not learn from him of these wonders. With a source of gold like this we can hire all the men we need. Get this machine working steadily and produce a good supply of this stuff. We must send out more recruiting agents and get our strength up. There will be plenty to do now, Saba."

"I thought you would find a use for this." Saba was very pleased that he saw the possibilities for everyone rather than as a means of getting rich. "It is a similar flow of slowed particles which make the matter progressively into heavier and heavier elements by the same method by which nature produced them in the first place; the intake of tiny particles of energy until the atoms build up into heavier atoms - the original process of transmutation which has produced every element from its tiny tenuous beginnings in space is here speeded up to utility by a concentration of the same basic material from which all matter grows. The Elder race was not stupid, was it?"

"No, Saba, we must work very hard to retrieve some of this mighty science for modern men."

## CHAPTER VI

### Preparation for Battle

MONTHS passed swiftly. A business-like activity, an atmosphere of industry, had replaced the lazy, secluded ways of the deserted hide-out of Eemeeshee.

## THE HIDDEN WORLD

Outside the big rock door in the cliff which gave entry to the underworld, the buildings of a mock gold mine gave them a cover for their gold production by the machine for transmutation. Also a cover for their recruiting activities.

Down in the caverns several thousand men now had their homes; practiced, drilled and studied steadily. They were swiftly reaching a point of full preparation for Eemeeshee's planned conquest of the caverns under Montana, and particularly those immediately under Butte.

The spider people, called in by the hundreds, had been treated with the beneficial energy flows from the ben-ray mech. Now, their faces sharpened in intelligence by its effects, they conducted scouting forces northward. Under their clicking, knowing guidance, the caverns were mapped, the roads carefully explored.

In the midst of this mapping work, Tch Tch and his "men" captured two of the enemy set to watch their activity. Lane, watching them taken to Eemeeshee for a going over, got a good idea of just who and what the enemy were.

The two men were dark, scrawny samples of humanity, in appearance like Paris Apaches or the criminal cockney type. But Lane saw, though they were human enough in general appearance, something had happened to their minds.

This became clearer as Eemeeshee augmented their thought within his telaug screens, watched their progress across the continent, their murder of everyone of the old ray groups they had found; a steady progress of conquest by silent murder of every intelligent bit of life they had found in the caves. Some of the people they had killed had solved the cryptic puzzles of the ancient writing and were fast winning for modern men the ancient writings of science which would have proved as valuable in time to man as man could have developed in many thousands of years of perfect progress. For the ancient metal records contained scientific method which it had taken a vastly superior race eons of time to perfect.

These murderous ignoramuses under their woman leader, Deliar Da Sylva, had wiped out many such quiet studious people in their uncomprehending grabbing for value, while the

1302

# THE HIDDEN WORLD

very murder by which they obtained gold and ancient stim mech wiped out knowledge worth infinitely more than the gain.

Both Eemeeshee and Lane had a pretty good understanding of what they were up against when the two captives died. Their opposition was a gang of ruthless and ignorant killers, who had for years been trying completely to wipe out all intelligent life in the underworld so that the whole mighty power of the underworld would be in their hands alone. That, in the process, they destroyed the whole future of men and set back progress another few thousand years, did not matter to them. They had no understanding of any duty toward other men. That, in the process, they had been destroying every surface man who knew of the antique world of wonder in the under-rock, did not matter to them; though many of these surface people "who knew" were the world's best medical research scientists and the health of millions of future men depended on their work. They were too ignorant to understand it was not self interest to kill a doctor, that one's own health depends on the health of medicine as a whole.

They had succeeded in their intention to wipe out all life in the sparsely inhabited caverns in the eastern states and had now progressed into the western caverns. Some few thousand people, intent on wiping out all life in an area bigger than the surface of the world - and succeeding due to the potent destructive power and vast range of the Elder race's weapons.

That was a terrible, a strange, weird scene: the death of these two murderous creatures. Standing before Eemeeshee, his vast form writhing like a great pudding bag, his great face with its long, upturned, outlandish nose peering down into their mind pictures augmented in a dozen screens before him, and behind the two terrified men the tall grey-white figures of the spider men, a dozen of them towering about the two men holding them there before Eemeeshee's great crystal machine home.

Eemeeshee's mind growing angrier and angrier as he summed up their bloody attempt to inherit the whole cavern

1303

world for themselves. Some million people, of the diverse and rather wonderfully informed kind that one finds sparsely scattered through the endless windings and tiers of the cavern world; men like Eemeeshee who had lived in the machines for centuries; men like Tch Tch who had evolved into a separate form of life, but whose clever fingers knew many a secret of the Elder science; people like Saba, who coupled with natural intelligence had had a lifetime of study under some centuries-old creature like Eemeeshee to become what man has always called the "sorceress' and worshipped; and the treasure hunters of the caverns - many, many of these they had killed by slow torture, wresting from their unwilling minds all their hard won secrets of the places where the Elder stores were hidden.

THE steady and successful progress of this attempt to inherit the whole ancient secret of the caves for one small group of a few thousand slavish robot-minded warriors, and their half dozen leaders such as the foremost, Deliar Da Sylva, dismayed and frightened Eemeeshee. But also gave him the courage of deperation.

Softly he pressed the stim button, lanced down a generously pleasant ray of stim-control upon the minds of the spider men, commanding them to kill these two bloody-minded captives. The gentle-natured spider men, without being able to help themselves, closed their long-fingered hands about the necks of these two from the far European Hellpits - and their breath soon stopped struggling to bring life to their bodies. Eemeeshee wanted the spider men to understand that all who lived bloodily as these men must die, and he wanted them to learn how to kill. The spider men left his presence wiser by a terrible intent to wipe out the Da Sylvas of the cavern world.

Lane looked down upon Eemeeshee's blue and gold and crystal nest of ancient technical wonder, the glory of its beauty marred - or enhanced - by the contrast of the tall weird spider men, dragging out the dead bodies of the two captives - and silently approved of Eemeeshee's resurgence of forgotten spirit. Had Lane been able fully to analyze the

1304

craven fear which had made Eemeeshee do this deed, and deprive the Legion of much needed information in one savage and fearful impulse to destroy an enemy, he would not have felt so approving of Eemeeshee. That ancient and complex brain was not a man's. Reading those minds had given Eemeeshee a terrible fear of this enemy that he must fight or die. He would fight, yes, because he must.

Lane turned to Saba, where she stood beside him watching the incongruity of the ancient wonder work and the peculiar and ugly life that moved about the mighty beauty of Eemeeshee's chamber.

"These allies of ours are not pretty, but they seem efficient."

"Eemeeshee should have preserved those lives for future reference," was all Saba said, and Lane did not notice her preoccupation. For Saba had noticed the craven fear in Eemeeshee and realized that all was not well with the great, pink-and-white and enormously ugly baby who was their leader. She inwardly resolved to keep an eye on future mental processes of that intricate and depraved brain that she served. Eemeeshee was a coward, she realized.

Eemeeshee's plans moved forward, driven by the desperation of Eemeeshee's full realization that the enemy was determined to wipe out all the older intelligents of the caverns, to have the whole cavern world as their private possession. Such an immense concept of selfishness had never been conceived by Eemeeshee. But he knew their project was possible with the Elder rays.

The day before their big push started northward, Lane dispatched a large packet of blueprints, plans and transcriptions from the Elder writings to a certain famous engineers club in California. His purpose was to leave in the hands of civilized men a full account of the affair if disaster overtook their attempt to reclaim the northern caverns for the red men. It would have saddened him to have seen the secretary of that club open his package.

The "educated" secretary read the explanatory letter carefully and consigned the whole packet of Elder wisdom to the wastebasket as the work of a deluded madman.

So many efforts of so many great men have been lost through the inability of "educated" men to give credence to any wisdom outside their limited "education." The plans and blueprints would have given modern men the secrets of the beneficial force flows, as well as the transmutation apparatus and the other mechanisms he had been able to understand and have blueprints drawn. But the "educated" secretary of the famous engineers club "knew" transmutation was "impossible."

This done, and his conscience free, his duty to the race of men fulfilled - he thought - Lane bent his energies to making of Eemeeshee's war a success. He knew that all their lives depended on winning this struggle; for flight would save none of them from the terrific range and sensitive detection of the Elder race machinery in the hands of murderers.

THAT advance! Those endless, vaulted halls extending on and on into every varying shifting translucent pearly color, pillared with rose and soft gleaming purples and transparent gold - endless shimmering beauty.

Aong the parallel gigantic roads, made to carry the vast traffic of a world packed with giant people of an energy and a titanic industry now lost to the mind of man (forever?); along those roads leading on and on into the mysterious beauties of a wonder land, rolled the weaponed, ray-armored cars of the ancients. Rolled? Floated! For the cars were half-spheres, floating on antigravity devices. Automatically they kept an unvarying height off the floor, the same height from the ceiling, no matter now many variations the construction had built into the way. A good thousand of these cars they had run out of the abandoned arsenal storerooms. Under Eemeeshee's instructions, learned to run them - and gold and the Red Legion had provided men to operate them, trained the men for the past months in their operation, in handling the titanic weapons built into the ancient war vehicles.

"How can such portable weapons fight the more massive fixed ray installations?" Lane had asked Eemeeshee.

## THE HIDDEN WORLD

"I will show you, for you must practice the maneuver so as to be able to form and strike simultaneously. See these markings on this huge stationary dynamo? That mark indicates the 'gens' or 'negs' of power the dynamo will generate. One kind of dynamo generates the beneficial 'gens' of energy, the other makes the 'negs' of detrimental weapon energy. Some dynamos marked with 'erg' generate a kind of mixture of both which has a multitude of uses, according to the nature of the mixture.* The number of these units indicates the range of the ray, the focus intensity being equal. This dial indicates the focus intensity of the beam, which you have already learned. Increasing the width of the beam decreases the range, as you know. As this machine is marked "one hundred gens" and the dynamos within the the anti-gravity cars are marked one gen or one neg it will take a hundred of such cars to equal the power of one such great fixed dynamo.

---

*Gen was an antique word meaning to create energy of a certain beneficial kind. Thus it had been adopted as the word for the unit of flow of beneficial energies from the dynamos designed to furnish the synthetic life-energy flows upon which the underworld life was based - as in our civilization upon the production of wheat. Thus "gen" was to their supply of life energy the word of unit as volt is to electric flow.

Neg was the reverse word unit, meaning unit of inverted destructive. De power. As volt is to electric, so is neg to energy flows which "negate" life. Note persistence of their word "neg" in our word "negate" to "neg" a "te" flow is to neutralize the life energies.

Erg is the word for unit of power of another kind. Between the opposed natures of gen and neg electric lie many in-between kinds of energy mixtures, as complex in nature as are compounds of molecular mixtures in chemistry to the element's relative simplicity. Mostly these are useless, and an erg is the unit of measurement for these mixture-flows. It is a unit used to indicate the degree of useless power mixed in their gen flows. Thus a current is 90 gen to ten erg; nearly pure life energy value in the creation of beneficial electric.

1307

"But the weapons within the cars are more finely built for fighting, more flexible of focus and can achieve much the same effect by amassing some seventy-five of their beams in one path. This can only be done by lining up the cars so that their beams strike through the same penetrative bore or guide ray, then their kinetic sum overcomes resistance of the same amount as the single beam of the giant dynamo. But there are only one or two such great dynamos in an arsenal. We can overcome a stationary ray installation by lining up more 'negs' of power than they have in their dynamos. Understand?"

"I follow you, Eemeeshee. It can be done by careful work."

"It can be done. There is this drawback: we cannot see so well with the small screens of these cars as with the larger power augmentation screen. They can see farther and better. But I have a way of providing us with equal sight. We have put the anti-gravs under some of the great vision screens, mounted the power units to operate it on other anti-grav units, connected them together with flexible cables – and, behold, we have portable vision quite as good as their stationary vision. Because the anti-gravs float exactly level, it is quite as satisfactory, for there is so little vibration in the anti-grav devices that even when in motion we can see nearly as well as a solid and stationary device. We will approach this enemy, stop at the utmost range we can see them, line up our weapon cars in exact simultaneous line of fire – and let them have it."

Eemeeshee was speaking with his abstract thought language which Lane had learned to interpret even more easily than English, as in fact, it is vastly a more potent medium of communication than oral language.

FOR the trip, Eemeeshee had squeezed his huge body into a smaller life-machine equipped with anti-gravs. When the central anti-grav is tipped slightly, it acts as a frictionless drive of great power. The gravity devices on the perimeter of the lower circle of the half-sphere are never moved from their exact alignment. These cars can travel

1308

## THE HIDDEN WORLD

at any speed the human eye and nerve can control within the caverns. They cannot be used outside the caverns without adjustment, as they have a device in their top that, like an electric eye, watches the ceiling and shuts off the anti-grav flow automatically, keeping the car a certain distance from the roof. Taken outside the cavern, this device would fail to work, the car would shoot straight up, unless the manual height control were understood and operated by hand.

Their long lines of floating cars, parallel and beautiful in their perfection of ancient workmanship, was fronted by Saba and Lane in a great vision ray-mech floated on anti-gravs. In the center of the lines was the great living machine of crystal and gleaming metal with Eemeeshee puffing inside. And in the rear were four smaller vision devices with Saba's women inside. Bringing up the rear was Stevens, inside the hugest hemi-sphere, a great single ray mech of longer range than any of the smaller cars. The larger part of the car was packed with small powerful dynamos, all powering a vast vision and firing beam in one compact unit. Eemeeshee had assured Stevens that nothing portable could outreach it. Their only danger, until they reached the location of the enemy under Butte, was from carelessness. If they failed to see some scouting ray and allowed it to get too close to their ranks, they would lose many men until the ray was put out of action.

Swiftly, silently, the tremendous assembly of ancient power floated northward. Here and there on the shimmering pearly beauty of the pillared ways hung a dried human head, giving mute evidence of the warfare of the degenerate, savage peoples who had peopled these caverns nomadically.

Or, a crucified mummy would hang from the great T symbol which the ancient Elder race had placed occasionally along the ways, just as today we see now and then the Christian cross which has derived from the ancient symbolic use of the T. The savages who had roamed here and perhaps fathered the present day spider-like "creeps," had left such evidences of their warring, and the dry warm air of the underworld had preserved the flesh perfectly, just as it had preserved the ancient machines and handiwork of the Elder race no matter the eon of time that had passed.

Eemeeshee's vast portable living machine was equipped with a mass of enigmatic apparatus. What it was all for, in truth, it is probable that even Eemeeshee did not know. But he certainly knew how to use most of it to advantage.

AS THEIR maps told them they were nearing ray field range, Eemeeshee shot forth a great grey beam of power far ahead of the advancing columns of war mech, and the results were startling. Lane speculated, as he watched the effects, just what the power-beam might be. He figured that the ray in some way altered the inner polarity of the basic building blocks of matter - the electronic polarity - so that it was no longer transparent to the penetray beams.

For, far ahead of their advance, the vision beams of penetrative ray had carefully revolved over the whole arc ahead, seeking for any sign of opposition. Now, as Eemeeshee played his ultra powerful beam of grey light ahead through the rock, the rock turned slowly grey and opaque to their vision beams, and they were advancing, instead of through apparent glass, through natural looking grey rock tunnels.

His purpose, evidently, was to keep the opposition's penetrative rays from finding their position. That it also obscured their own means of sight troubled Lane. But the purpose of the ancient being in the great crystal complexity floating weirdly in their midst became clearer as Eemeeshee shut off the grey beam. Now, as they neared the farther edge of the cloudlike greyness he had created within the rock, their own penetray beams became able to peer out ahead - while themselves were invisible within the opacity of the rock. Lane halted his floating car just within this area of opacity, and waited, searching far ahead with his vision beam, watching his screen with great care for the slightest sign of enemy preparation.

For what seemed forty miles ahead the ways led, parallel, empty of life - the alien splendor of the construction glistening here and there where walls and vertical construction had kept the usual blanket of time's dust from forming. Even through that pall of eons of slow precipitation of dust the lovely forms of the machine art of the ancients showed, row on row, arrangement on arrangement, chamber after chamber, tier on tier of vast, waiting perfection - waiting always for the feet of those immortal Elder masters who would never return to this death-laden planet.

Of the modern interlopers within these sacred halls, there was no sign. No breath of a ray trail, no slightest bristling ionizing of the dust layer betrayed with its stirring a watch ray. Not even a footprint upon that dust, not one tread of the magnetic anti-grav beams upon the dust-layer left its tell-tale path before them. Apparently no life had touched these endless tunnels and God-built chambers since they were abandoned so long ago. Yet their maps told them that hereabout were the forces who had taken over the caverns under Montana. That hereabout must lie swift and terrible destruction for them if unwary.

Slowly they crept forward, their watch rays sweeping, sweeping, and Eemeeshee's mysterious beam changing the polarity of the rock ahead of them so that themselves remained invisible to any penetray beam from the distance. Lane realized that this opacity yielded to their own beams because close to the source such a beam is vastly more powerful than at its tenuous further end. He appreciated Eemeeshee's abilities, for this hiding of themselves within a field of opacity in the rock was in truth clever.

"I hope Eemeeshee has a few more tricks up his sleeve against these European ray. God knows what they may use against us," Lane murmured to Saba. She smiled reassuringly.

"The old one is really enjoying himself for the first time in my life time. I would not believe he could change so. You have done him much good; I would pit his ancient heritage of wisdom from the strange people who fathered him against any bunch of modern murderers. These who set upon your Red Legion and drove them out; we know more about them than you think. They have killed and tormented the 'creeps'; some of the spider men had fled westward to tell me of them. Also the nomads have told me of them. We know

1311

nomads have told me of them. We know what they are, and we know how they fight. But behind them may be some old behemoth from the past who may not be such easy prey. Eemeeshee is not the only old one in the caves."

Cautiously the long columns of floating cars crept ahead with the care of troops penetrating a minefield. When death comes from ray, it comes lancing swiftly out of unseeable distance, and the swiftest only is life left. To the first who sighted the enemy, to them came the advantage; and they meant to be the first.

## CHAPTER VII

### The Battle Is Joined

NOW, quite suddenly, they saw life ahead. Like a telescopic view of an anthill, the distance making them so tiny, and the penetrative rays making all the rock about the far off titan burrows like so much glass. They saw the city of the intruders.

This was what once had been the home of the lost tribe of Votan Indians; Indians inheriting all the pride and culture of a race more advanced than the Mayan plus the knowledge of science that centuries of life in the wonder caverns of the Elder race had given them. The ancient original beauty of the place was overhung with the semi-barbaric trappings, the feathered head-dresses, the blankets woven in bizarre and ancient symbolic patterns, woven by nimble fingered squaws here where all the beauty of the Elder work inspired to greater understanding of the nature of beauty than ever surface red men rose to acquire. Pelts of wolf and hides of deer, the fleeces of sheep and the hides of bear decorated the ancient spring-metal couches and softened the polished stone to the foot.

Sprawled amid this semi-barbaric Indian splendor were some few hundred European aliens, clad in modern clothing, loud jackets and slacks; gaudy silk dresses from surface shops. On the women, bare white shoulders aped surface luxury, while waiting on them were the Indians who had

## THE HIDDEN WORLD

lived and ruled secretly here up to their advent. Lane knew they had not been here more than two years. Hugging the hope that their short tenure had not given them time to get fully acquainted with all the resources and weapons of the intricately chambered tiers of caverns, Lane swung the nozzle of his dis-cannon* in line with his vision penetray, prepared to fire when the others were aligned to fire with him.

Stim rays bathed the great chambers where the white newcomers lolled, apparently engaged in a debauch. The Indians, clad in loin cloths or in grey linen jackets and skirts which seemed to be a kind of servant's uniform, bore drinks and food; or stood stony faced, as door tenders; or pushed mop and bucket along the endless corridors.

For entertainment, one of the gaudier females was crushing the eight-foot, stick-like limbs of a "creep" inch by inch with a hammer; two men held his piteously screaming form while she plied the hammer and the rest looked on. Evidently this was great sport. Lane ground his teeth at the needless, purely wanton cruelty. Lane had much to learn of the nature of these people.

In the great war-ray chamber near at hand to the lolling

---

*These dis-cannon are of several varied kinds. Mostly they have a dial which controls atunement, and fire over a penetrative conductive "lead" as vision ray which conducts the destructive bolt but is not itself harmful in any way. The control dial alters the nature of the dis-bolt so that it can be slowly changed through a long series of intensities, from mildly warm to harmful "de" to straight dis, which latter and worst will melt a hole through the rock for many miles, or kill if held there for a short time. This "de" is a detrimental ray used for many purposes, originally designed apparently for such purposes as an insecticide - it can be set to sweep a great area with diffuse beams of mildly destructive power, or concentrated into a stronger beam one shot of which upsets a man's mind into temporary insanity.

1313

sybarites who ruled the place, were the stub fingered ray ro.*

Lane had learned from Saba that the ancients' word for the magnetism between sexes - between man and woman - was "ne." He had observed this animal magnetism that binds all humanity together in an electrical matrix, over the telaug beams which augment all these subtle electrical flows into mental vision strength. He had realized that "ne" was a most important part of life, making it much more interesting than it would be without. Now, watching these newcomers to this part of the caverns, he realized that the character signs - the variant-natured "ne" charge which each physical body exerts upon each other physical body - were either missing from their bodies, or so vague as hardly to register mentally even with the mighty augmentation of the ancient power tubes. Instead there was present a repellance ("ne" is an attraction) which acted in an exactly opposite manner to "ne." Instead of liking each other, admiring or respecting their most capable and best looking members, they hated each other, and this hatred was in direct proportion to their ability and appearance.

Lane realized that here was revealed the reason for their characters being cruel and evil; the reason for their constant and savage warring.

Saba glanced at him as he observed this startling difference, which was so obvious over the telaug beams with

---

*These are men found around any of the dero "bunches." Men who have been used by "make-ray" (ray control) to fire the more detrimental of the huge old rays; used in warfare until their fingers rot off from X-ray infection; until their minds cease to exist as anything but unnecessary adjunct. They are often huge men, drafted into such service for their size and strength, and never thereafter allowed any freedom. They wait in their ray-chambers just as the great old mechanisms wait - until it is time for action. Then the "make-rays" reach in, seize their poor minds and direct them in the battle.

**1314**

# THE HIDDEN WORLD

which they were observing the enemy.

"The Elder word for that is "de," she told him. "It makes the difference between human and destructive beast."

As Lane swung his telaug beam across the ray-mutilated stalwarts waiting in the war-ray chambers, he observed that this "de" was even more strongly present among them. He guessed its presence was due to the effects of the destructive rays created by the great ray-cannon, effects which destroyed the "ne" generative inner life of the cells leaving an animal whose life could hardly be a life thereafter, since even the love he bore a woman turned to hate in his breast. He observed that only habits of discipline kept these great, dull-eyed men from throwing themselves upon each other in a struggle to the death. An explanation of the real cause of men's terrible and constantly recurring wars was here presented to Lane's eyes. But Lane saw no solution to it at first glance, other than shielding all men from such natural occurring rays by some kind of dielectric sheathing for their cities which would keep out such "de" generating rays.

BUT Lane did not have much time for speculative thought, for Eemeeshee was swiftly preparing for action. The floating hemi-spheres of smaller ray-cannon cars were lining up, one behind the other, under swiftly darting telaug beams bearing his thought to each driver.

Lane could not help dreading the first clash for he realized that their attack upon this huge citadel with their small rays was apparently foolhardy, and that none of them but Eemeeshee and possibly Saba really could evaluate the situation in military terms.

Somehow Lane could not feel a great deal of confidence in Eemeeshee after old Secumne's analysis of him. Would

---

For a picture of what the underworld has always been to surface men, read "The Silver Nail" by Carmen Sylva (the Queen of Roumania) and Alma Strettell. There are several pertinent tales in her important book - "Legends from River And Mountain."

his resurgence of interest in life remain or would he suddenly sink again into the apathy and dream-making with which he had wasted so many years - how many centuries, Lane wondered?

Saba hissed in almost inaudible tones.

"Look at those 'courageous' animals who could fight their way through a group of unarmed children, themselves unseen, and with these terrible weapons from a distance wipe out the young humans - and often have. Are they not wonderful, agh?"

Lane looked over her ray screen, and sent his own beam along its invisible direction sensing its path with his telaug ear. Soon he heard and saw the leaders of this invasion.

"Mrs. Da Sylva, may I get a drink?"

A young and pretty slave girl stood in her worn rags near the door, evidently she could not leave her position except by permission.

The woman's answer, "Later!" told Lane enough; the girl had to remain standing there thirsty. He knew automatically she would not get her drink till her duty period ended. He swung his ray a trifle to take in this Da Sylva.

About her incredibly huge waist strained a glittering girdle of fine metal work. In the girdle was caught many shining loops of dark transparent satin that Lane realized had never been woven by modern hands or machines; it was too beautiful material. Through the beautiful stuff her heavy thighs, the great hips, gleamed grossly.

The barrel of her body projected starkly nude above the girdle, burly and strong as a man, and two strips of gleaming black mesh broadened over her terrific breasts - Broadening over the gross lushness like the great buds of two horribly fecund flowers. Something of the ugly attraction of death was in her. She exuded a passion of cruelty.

The great strong rounds of her shoulders were shining naked. This stark, gross parody of womanhood stood there, too vividly outlined by the mellow, age-old beauty of the Elder chamber, and the medusa coils of her black hair framed a face of heavy, almost masculine beauty. The

1316

sensuous, too-full lips, an aquiline nose - she looked the female pirate to perfection.

In Lane's mind her wide red mouth, those dark horrible depths of her eyes, the black magic of her cruel face was printed in bitter ink forever.

Her words were directed to a milder edition of herself, seated nearby and peering intently at something taking place in the distance which she was watching over the old ray screen.

"I married him, the tout, and he took me to the caves."

"I guess you soon turned the tables on him, eh, Deliar?"

"Precious right I did. I soon had the big-shot wound around my finger, and it wasn't long till he died and left me in charge. We have come a long way since then, haven't we, Miro?"

"We have managed to abolish these red dupes' ideas of freedom, and made a paying machine out of their labor, and their mines. We have overcome the best and oldest of the dreaded Eastern rays; the goody, goody things that they were! And now this rich western area lies open to us."

"When we get this area lined up to production, we will move southward. I have heard of some great stores of the Elder treasures under California."

STANDING behind Miro, the Da Sylva woman watched her, then said:

"Give that loafing workman a little 'sinus' through the the soles of his feet; he has been laying down on the job."

Manipulating a pain ray through the screen before her, Miro laid the man upon the mine's floor with pain, he lay there writhing and shrieking with the sudden attack. As the pain ceased, he got up and seized his shovel, began to labor with a great show of industry. What else could he do?

"That's what these lazy b - need, a dose of pain to tell them they are not anything but dogs to us. They will learn to work!"

Lean-ribbed from poor food and pale from the underworld lack of sun, the workmen labored on, nor looked up at the screams and commotion of the one punished. They wore

1317

regular blue denim, ragged and soiled, in their miner's caps the regular miner's lamp hung. It was some ancient boring now being worked again, and by the looks it was gold, and very rich.

It was a white quartz vein, heavily shot with the yellow stuff. The vein was all of twelve feet wide. The men worked in a heavy silence. Fear rode them was apparent.

Behind Lane, Eemeeshee's preparatory tactical rearrangement seemed about finished. As his ray swept up to them, Saba pointed out Da Sylva's central chamber, where the power of this place seemed to have its home. Eemeeshee took a good look, and Lane could hear his "Hah!" of disgust and a kind of solemn glee in him at the set-up. Lane knew he was thinking, "This is going to be a cinch." Lane hoped he was right.

Suddenly from two miles overhead a cream-colored ray shot down through the blackness, and the "ulegra" (Elder word for electric) flowed over the ray, into the war-ray chambers where the rows of great-bodied, dull-faced fighting ro waited, animating them for the emergency that the watch ray far overhead had sensed, having observed the grey opacity with which Eemeeshee had surrounded his columns.

In seconds the grey cloud around them was shot through with the flaming disbeams from the great war-ray mech. They weren't connecting, for Eemeeshee had caused a great area of the rock to become opaque, but they were searching out the area with a systematic thoroughness that left no room for doubt that they would score a hit soon or late.

Eemeeshee's great unturned caricature of a nose, lumpy and grotesque, flamed beet red with excitement. His vast, pillow-soft white body quivered like a grub on a fish-hook as he waved both hands at the watching rays of his columns of ray-spheres to fire and keep firing. His excited thought struck fear into Lane, for he was too much like some womanish officers he had seen, who lose all self control in emergency.

But the columns of Indian-manned ray-cars began to pull the steady-fire studs on their instrument panels, and their thousand rays were soon lashing out in perfect, irresistible

1318

alignment toward the huge war-ray chamber where the great mutilated bodies of the ro-ray men moved machine-like above the great cannon, sweeping the vast and deadly nozzles directing dis-flow rays in searching patterns through the opaque cloud that was Eemeeshee's position.

Almost to the source of those flaming beams our own beams reached, but not quite. Something was wrong, Eemeeshee's beams were not reaching, not striking down those dull-faced robots. Saba added her own huge ray to the multiple beam, and the glowing transparent path of the ray moved within a few short feet of the vast mechanisms that were blasting at them with the terrible energies created by that forgotten race.

Now down from that female leader Da Sylva's luxurious chamber a ray reached in upon those laboring robots, searching their minds for their almost non-existent thoughts as she looked for a way to reach the attackers within their impenetrable opacity. A premonition of failure, a feeling that if they were going to win this fray and live through it they had better do something in a hurry. Lane shot a telaug ray back at Eemeeshee, but the old loafer was slumped in a dead faint! Excitement had proved too much for him!

Lane looked at Saba. Her flushed, worried face told him she had seen what had happened to their champion from the past. In spite of himself Lane had to grin at the big booby fainting on them.

Nearer and nearer the searching, criss-crossing dis-rays reached toward their columns. Lane knew it was a matter of seconds before they found the Red Legion with death. To make matters worse, the terrific power of their dis-rays was turning the opaque rock back to normally transparent polarity, the penetrays guiding the beams made the searched parts of the great cloud in the rock as clear as glass. This made it much easier for the dull-minded robots to keep their systematic search pattern.

Saba swung open the disc of the door, leaped out into the great tunnel, raced backward to the huge crystalline floating structure in which the unconscious Eemeeshee lay, his great lips curved in the sensual, childish expression of pleasure

1319

which was habitual to him and to all who are slaves to the dream-mech habit. Lane guessed he was living over some of the dreams of infinite pleasure which had wasted his centuries old life.

The lithe Indian girl clawed her way into the complexities of the interior, hurled her soft lovely body in unaccustomed violent exertion toward the controls of that vast ancient machine of Eemeeshee's where must lie their only salvation, if there were any for them. Even as she sought for the way into Eemeeshee's air-tight living chamber, the master beam of the war-ray from the enemy's robotic humans found the tail end of their column, began to blot from existence the crystal bubbles, which broke and melted under the mighty power of destruction as if in truth but bubbles of nothingness.

## CHAPTER VIII

### Desperate Charge

DELIAR DA SYLBA turned to her companion.

"There goes another danger - up in smoke. So will they all. I am curious as to just who and what that column of mech is, anyway. I had not thought another power like our own in strength existed in all the western caverns."

Miro smiled in relief at her mistress. Then she turned back to watch the terrible power of the flaming dis-ray eating steadily at the long, now revealed column of ray-cars. She clenched and unclenched her long-fingered, red-nailed hands until blood streamed from the palms. It had been a close thing and they both knew it.

"Tonight we will have our fill of killing, the survivors will certainly enjoy themselves while they learn who it was they attacked."

"When you've sated your pleasure, may I then kill some of them my own way?" asked Miro, her gross face owl-hungry, her fleshy lips curling back over her teeth redly, a slight drool on her chin.

The great dis-ray which had been rubbing out the

1320

floating cars, completely destroying the occupants, was now changed by Da Sylva's order to a concussive vibratory ray which merely laid out the occupants unconscious. She wanted her meat alive for the "fun" to follow. Swiftly the rays swept over the endlessly long columns.

\* \* \*

"ADVANCE," screamed Saba over the great telemach with which Eemeeshee had maintained contact with the columns. It was their only salvation to pull forward those few feet needed for their beams to reach that center of the vast machines where sourced the beams destroying them.

As one man, the Indians, spurred to quick obedience by Saba's shriek, swung forward the levers of the anti-grav generators and the remaining few hundreds of ray-cars swept forward, down upon the flaming source of the death. Now their beams, weakened to less than effective strength, reached the chamber, but failed to stop the living, mutilated gargoyles within the chamber from their ray-driven robot work. On and on they plunged toward the death-dealing master-ray, and swiftly the great vibratory beams lashed at them.

Saba now pressed all the studs she knew anything about on the great organ-like keyboard of Eemeeshee's weapon car, and the beams reached out toward the war-ray chamber where the ray-ro toiled like maddened devils swinging the great controls of the master mech - for they were built for men three times the modern height.

Saba downed the "ro" at the great lever of the master-beam, one by one they fell as she flung back her hair from her flaming face and strained every muscle at the great machine's levers. Clumsily the huge beam swept about the chamber, striking the laboring ro more by chance than by skill. The whole smoking and scream-filled chamber fell into near darkness as the big human robots dropped in death and their weight, dropped releasingly from the levers, let the great, whining dynamos slow into an idling hum.

Saba started her search of the whole area for the other war-ray posts which she knew must be manned; must be readying themselves for attack.

Following her lead, the red men at the smaller ray controls sent their beams lancing out in a terrific criss-cross of searching rays - for there were several hundred of them still in untouched condition. All about lay their comrades, some charred and still-smoking corpses, others in a trance like death from the concussion of the vibratory ray sat at their ray-mech switch-panels like frozen men, staring straight ahead, or slumped in retching paralysis from the effects of other beams.

Now, seeing the mighty mass of ray still searching for them, the Da Sylva ray-ro, stationed far above her chambers* in desperation gave up their silence and darkness which had protected from this sudden assault and staked their chances on a sudden lashing attack with their long distance ray-needles. (These are very thin pencils of ray whose very narrowness makes the power needed to activate them much less, and the "carry" of the ray is much farther.)

---

*In the ancient war-ray arrangement of ray chambers, the ray-mech are grouped about a central master ray in concentric rings of eight or ten tiers of levels, making a hundred to two-hundred ray chambers disposed in a cylindrical shape with the master ray at the center. Modern dwellers in the caverns usually man but some half-dozen of these ancient chambers, and are able to use but two or three percent of the mechanisms installed in the vast chambers. But to search the intricacies of the great old defensive setup took time.

---

In the story "Masked World," I described the use of a teleport for purposes of attaining immortality. I want to tell you this use of the teleport is purely invention. To my knowledge the teleport leaves nothing behind, is not safe for transportation of life any distance - though it might be so in capable hands. Most teleportations of humans result in amnesia or total insanity. Will try to label in stories which uses of antique mech are correct and which are invention. - R.S.S.

1322

## THE HIDDEN WORLD

These fiery needles of death reaching down at them from a half dozen points in the darkness overhead, began to pick off the red men one by one, the fiery needles searching swiftly through their bodies till a fatal spot was found. (The pain of such a death is excruciating, for the needles are not fatal unless they pierce the heart or cut the spinal column at the base of the brain.) Steadily these needles lanced through their flesh, searching inexorably for their heart strings; while Saba with Eemeeshee's master mech ray searched the miles of darkness overhead for the source of the needles.

One by one, under the fierce-eyed, sweating girl's swift desperate hands, the far, fiery lances of death ceased to plague them, and at last the whole area before their advance fell silent and dark.

Now again Saba called into the augment mech her command, "Advance!" and again the levers plunged forward, their cars lifted slightly and slid forward faster, faster, into the heart of the web of caverns where laired that evil acquisitiveness, that cruel, fleshy female thing Lane had seen for short moments before the attack began.

AS THEY slid silently forward in the darkness Lane was thinking of a newspaper item he had seen a month before of a treasure of two billion dollars of bullion hidden by the Japanese in the waters of Tokyo bay. He connected their victory, inexperienced and inept as it had been, with this item in the papers. For if ray personnel and information and power was as all-embracing and wonderfully powerful and intelligent as some devotees of the secret rays say (and believe) he knew that two billion would not have lain there all that time it did. Too, if such as this Da Sylva had been doing her duty by the allies, instead of plundering along underground, she could have been in Japan; her rays would have seen this information of the two billion dollars bullion sunk in the harbor, and she would have acquired the money, for no one but the Japs knew it was there for months. He wondered how many proud and lazy ray were cursing their timid failure to invade Japan with the surface soldiers,

1323

when they read this item of missed loot in the papers.

But then, it might have been some loyal young fighter like Saba who had uncovered the stuff for the Yank soldiers. And it might have been their absence from the home caverns that laid the ancient place open to such as Da Sylva, their absence fighting on the front; unseen, unknown, unheralded - but fighting with the vast ancient mystery mech for their country which did not even know they existed. It was hard to reconcile their activities, if that was true, with their continued deprivation of such medically valuable information from suffering people the world over. This ancient secret, this time-forgotten monopoly, why did it go on? Lane looked back at Eemeeshee, snoring peacefully in his dream, and knew why.

Because those time-pampered, God-mech raised creatures who should have been like Gods; worshipped pleasure - were raised never to make an effort by the ancient all-providing living machines.

The Elder race must have had some stimulus from nature or from their own wisdom that the past of such as Eemeeshee did not have in their life. Else they would not have been the Elder race; they would have been such as Eemeeshee, and they would never have produced the mech that had made life so easy for Eemeeshee, and there would have been no Eemeeshee, and no necessity for struggling against the more evil groups of the caverns.

## CHAPTER IX

### Victory for the Red Legion

AS THEY advanced, fire from the remaining outposts kept harrassing them. Not hitting much, but dangerously close, firing blindly as they were through Eemeeshee's opacity ray making the rock impervious to the penetray vibrants. Slowly, steadily, they found the source of those rays and wiped them out with flashing blasts of flaming energy through the resisting rock.

They could hear Da Sylva screaming thought-orders, her

thought-voice like a banshee's anger in her desperation. It was a good feeling to hear that cruel voice facing death. It was good to know she was not relishing the last pangs of some long-tortured "creep" or slave human worker of hers.

At last she, too, fell unconscious under a bolt from Saba's ray, and the far outposts fell silent. They could hear over the telaug beams their frantic thoughts as they scrambled into the gravity defying hemispheres and shot away along the great cavern roads. Half their forces set out in pursuit, the other half made sure there were no traps, and took over Da Sylva's central chamber and her own garishly revulsive self.

Eemeeshee looked long and ponderingly upon Deliar Da Sylva's sleek, yet gross and revolting body. Her fate, what should it be, what could he do to punish her, as Eemeeshee's enemies were supposed to be punished of old time?

The others under Saba's swift thought-voice supervision took over the controls of the central master rays and swept the whole cavern labyrinth with a vast crisscross of seeking rays to make quite sure that the fight was really over and no man lying out in the dark for one overturning treacherous sweep of deadly ray when all their "shorter" ray fans were off and they were unsuspecting.

Lane had time for one long sigh of relief, realizing that the fear that had plagued and killed his Red Legion was now gone. But why, why had Da Sylva sent killers on the trail of the Legion? Lane resolved to find out!

Lane sent his own telaug beam from his floating car upon Da Sylva's now half-conscious head. As that awful sub-conscious thought was augmented into overwhelmingly loud impulses within his mind a terrible revulsion at even hearing what she thought took place. It was like reading Satan's mind, if Satan was a woman.

The things she had done, the terrible ideas that showed now to Lane as great images of reality of the past, were filtered and changed by time, but augmented by the telaug into reality again. The scenes of her past fascinated him as a bird is fascinated by a snake, for Lane did not know that the telaug cannot be used at too great strength for long periods without hypnosis, or he had forgotten Saba's warning in his first shocked mental immersion into evil female thought now taking place within his own mind more strongly than his own pale unaugmented thought. It was strange to feel oneself a woman, an evil, passionate, lusting, cruel and bloody woman with a past that Bluebeard would have envied. Strange and fascinating, for the joy of her mind in her past was relived by Da Sylva as she realized she had not long to live. Thankfully came her thought.

"Anyway, I got mine while the getting was good!"

SUDDENLY into that garishly distorted beauty where the handiwork of this Da Sylva bunch had managed to alloy the original ancient beauty and the barbaric Indian additions of a different kind of charm with an overlay of modern gaudiness; into that scene of victory and vengeance came a mighty voice over a green beam of terrific power.

"Eemeeshee, I am Mexitli. You have brought war to people under my protection. I must kill you, Eemeeshee, even though you are of the old race. I cannot allow this insult.

Eemeeshee, whose beet-red apoplectic face had resumed its normal pallor through his unconscious fit and his subsequent awakening to a victory he had failed to contribute much to winning, suddenly went a beet red again, his great arms began to quiver, his lips to drool and tremble. Even Lane could see through the common ray trick, but the mighty Eemeeshee - no, he had to believe everything he heard. Some fleeing enemy had decided to make one more try at besting them - had flung an unobserved telaug beam into the chambers of Da Sylva and had carefully searched Eemeeshee's mind for his one greatest fear. Finding this fear in his memories of some feared enemy of the past, he had imitated the nature of this Mexitli - the voice at first - and now into the chamber came a great solidograph projection of the figure of this fake "Mexitli". Even Lane understood the nature of the ruse. This new enemy had seen the image in Eemeeshee's thought, had caught the thing with the antique thought recorder attachment, was now reprojecting

1326

## THE HIDDEN WORLD

the image from Eemeeshee's own mind. But not Eemeeshee – oh no. If some one said something, he had to believe it.

Lane understood now why Secumne had been so discouraged with the character of these creatures of Eemeeshee's kind. His great face purple with fear and upset circulation, his trembling hands sought the great control levers of his crystal mechanism. The anti-gravs lifted it, slowly at first, then rapidly, the great shining machine floated off down the corridor, swung into the wide ways toward the south. Deaf to all their shouted entreaties over their rays as they watched this craven flight of their leader from a mere voice and projection, Eemeeshee's great floating temple of forgotten machinery began to speed away from them, was soon lost to their following search rays.

Meanwhile Saba, taking it all in with a half smile of sad understanding on her face, swung the huge rays from the war-ray chamber of Da Sylva's where she had remained with four stalwarts of the Legion to insure that the great old mech were properly manned. Swung them searching the distance for the origin of this fake voice and picture which had cost them their leader. Swung them, and, with gathering doubt and indecision on her face, failed to find the source.

Something that Eemeeshee was thinking as he fled puzzled Lane.

"Mexitli is a messenger from Apollo. Mexitli is an Apollo."

"Just what did Eemeeshee mean by mentioning Apollo? Just what did Eemeeshee mean by mentioning the name Apollo? How could he know anything about a God moderns think Greek?" Saba turned to Lane, saying,

"I will show you our Apollo records from the past. Apollo was a God known all over earth when he was here, and he is well known to Eemeeshee from his dream life – which is made up of records, is in truth a reliving of the ancient God life. That is why he is so frightened. The coming of Mexitli is to him a sign of Apollo's anger. He would not be frightened, but long immersion in the record dream life has made him unable to think of such things as in the past. To him they are very much today, and he is frightened of Mexitli who was a very vengeful follower of Apollo. Sometime I will show you records of that time when Apollo was on earth."

"All that is not much help to us. We are now in grave danger without Eemeeshee's help to us. Whoever is doing the faking that scared Eemeeshee off must have some idea of following up the fake with an attack. We've got to find him first."

"We shall." Saba was grim, and her women hastened about on her thought orders, too fast for Lane to hear or understand what she was telling them.

NOW, from the projection of the terrible figure of Mexitli, a tall black-feathered giant of horrific aspect, his mouth a great, fanged cavern in his painted face, his hands holding strange instruments - from this grotesque figure from the far past of the Amerind domination of cavern life - came streamers of pale fire out upon them. Stronger and stronger grew these pale streamers of fire, and pain and heat began to drive them back from proximity to the great and growing, solid-seeming apparition.

Saba shouted to Lane.

"Do not fear or flee. If he could kill with the mech he has activated he would do so. He may cause pain and discomfort, but I doubt he can kill - or he would."

Again that terrible voice from the past flung its weird thought-pictures at us from the apparition, saying:

"One every day. Now it will be one every minute, till you flee again as before. I am not what you think. Die, dogs of Indians, die! You are not men. Your leader flees. You are shameless cowards. Flee! Flee!"

Even as Lane absorbed the abstract message and made it into words in his mind, a long streamer wrapped around Stevens from head to foot. He dropped to the floor, writhing and shrieking in agony. Lane leaped forward, seized Stevens' shoulders, dragged him back from the pale, painful fire of the rays.

They had not bothered to bind or imprison the woman Da Sylva or her companion, and in the chamber with Lane were only Saba, Stevens and two or three of the Red Legion. They had depended on the many ray beams from the ray chambers they had occupied on holding such captives. For it is impossible for a person to run away from a ray; its vast range makes the attempt somewhat like that of an ant trying to run away from a tidal wave. It just can't be done.

But with Eemeeshee fleeing in the distance, and most of the ray mech engaged in hunting for the source of the Mexitli projection, Da Sylva heaved her heavy body into one of the empty half-spheres, followed by Miro, and made the attempt anyway. They did not notice her till she was some distance down the long corridor leading to the ancient highway toward the north.

Lane sprang to the stationary ray installation in the big chamber and sent Da Sylva's own ray after her, flashed a bolt into the drive mech of the car, stopped it, smoking, dead, about a mile down the corridor. Other than that, they found no time to bother with the two women, left them trudging on foot toward the highway. They would have time later to pick them up. Meanwhile this new menace had to be dealt with.

Da Sylva found another abandoned grav-car and made good her escape - thanks to the confusion. They were to pay for their carelessness with this she-scorpion.

SABA at last traced the tenuous projection beam to its source. Lane, watching, was puzzled to find several ragged, dirty workmen in a great ray chamber, manipulating the telesolidograph expertly. Saba sent a telaug beam into the chamber asking,

"Who are you?"

In their minds the anwer "Votan warriors" flashed inadvertently and Saba shouted in sudden glad understanding. These were some of the original Indian people who had held these caverns before the advent of Da Sylva; had not known of the retiring Eemeeshee far to the north; did not recognize the men of the Red Legion as allies. Able to kill, they yet were thankful to the Red Legion for driving out Da

Sylva and freeing them, but at the same time they saw an opportunity to wrest from this struggle their old supremacy and had sent the projection of Mexitli into the chamber to frighten off Eemeeshee.

Their cunning analysis of Eemeeshee's nature and the effectiveness of their bug-a-boo in accomplishing their object were interesting to us, but Saba explained that we had come only to set them free; had no designs on their possessions or homes.

Soon they joined Saba in Da Sylva's central chamber and helped to enlist the others of the surviving Votan who were found fleeing their bondage in all directions, now that their cruel guards had gone.

That night found the whole system of caverns under this area of Montana under our domination, and the slow swinging watch-rays covering every great old tunnel road from the north and east; others watching too the other highways in case danger came from some of the Da Sylva outfit who might have circled to attack again from some unexpected direction. But all seemed quiet, and it was a triumphant Red Legion and a rejoicing band of Votan ex-slaves who bedded down that night in those magnificent old chambers. Da Sylva had made good her escape, and they thought no more of her. But should have, for Da Sylva was not through. In the middle of the night a choking sensation waked Saba, her eyes in the darkness unnaturally sensitized by some fear, saw, as only Saba could see in such darkness by some sixth sense, the clouds of strange choking gas flooding the chambers, billowing down the corridors. She leaped to the great vision screen and sent the central master ray of the great fortification circling in search of this strange threat.

It was true. Billowing down the corridors from the north came a strange gas, and choking and gasping, fleeing before the rolling billows of death, came the hundreds of Votans who had bedded in the northern chambers; came also the men set to watch the northern guard rays in their automatic sweep of the northern highways. Comprehension came swiftly to Saba, and she woke all the sleeping men, swiftly told them to prepare to flee from their hard-won victory. Lane standing

1330

## THE HIDDEN WORLD

now beside Saba, seeking a way to understand what was happening, heard her mutter:

"The teleports - she left one in these caverns set to receive, made her way northward during the distraction of the Votan attack, and now, as we sleep, has placed some ancient gas from the storerooms of the Elder race into the sending chamber of some abandoned teleport in the northern ways, sending into our area vast quantities of the ancient gas. Luckily it does not seem very deadly..."

Lane answered her unconscious speech.

"The gas is cyanogen chloride. It is deadly enough if it is insupportable. Can you not blow it back upon them in some way? Are there no air pumps, nothing to rid ourselves of the gas? What are you saying of teleports? I do not understand..."

"There is no time. If we had time, we could set men at getting the ancient pumps in running order to clear the air, but with the gas rolling down upon us, all I say is flee while there is time. As the gas dissipates, we can return to these caverns as quickly as Da Sylva. She must think us fools to think that we will not."

OVER her telaug, swiftly flashing from group to group of our men, Saba gave the order to evacuate immediately.

That retreat, heartsick at their losses, plagued by the pursuing demoniacs under Da Sylva's raging thought-voice control whipping them to suicidal efforts to reach them with their equally ranged weapons, made their efforts to protect their rear costly. Steadily the Red Legion paid for their temerity in attacking Da Sylva - with their blood. Continually the fleshy, vengeful witch sacrificed mindless ro after ro to get within range, shoving a mass of speeding floating spheres ahead here while over there in adjacent parallel corridors, overhead, or deep underneath, sped forward single ray-cars in an endeavor to distract their watch-ray from one or the other long enough to get in a shot.

Da Sylva's numbers, steadily augmented by her now returning men, speeding up from the far-flung frontiers of

1331

her holdings to take their place in the battle line, were now equal to their own. And their inexperience proved no match for the mindless ro, who under control from the many control beams from the cars of Da Sylva's henchmen, were each as capable in handling the ray as the veterans controlling their thought.

Steadily their losses grew, car by car they fell into smouldering wreckage, faster and faster the panic stricken Red Men fled before them.

Silently Lane cursed the non-existent spine of the great old bag of wind, Eemeeshee.

"Breath-Master" indeed! He must have gotten that name from bragging of exploits he was too timid to have done, or from his short-winded and continual puffing over the augmented telaug beams, heard by the Indians of the surface long ago, rather than from any mastery of the winds of fate and the heavens as he had supposed.

Death flamed after them from near a thousand lances of the red-flaming dis-needles, and ever and again one of his loyal Red Legion shrieked as the needles sought through his body for a fatal spot. On they fled, the levers setting the anti-grav beams into the forward-driving slant in the last notch. Nothing but the auto-ray eyes controlled them from plunging into the curves of the cavern ways. The silent, gleaming dust-laden beauty of the mighty, earth crust supporting pillars of the hardened rock of the Elder's creation fled past them in terrible rushing rows, the eye could not follow the whirling march of the pillared, time-heavy vastness past into the dark.

Steadily Lane searched the backward trail with his beam at full extension focus, firing, firing, and at every blast some car of Da Sylva's flamed into hurtling fiery death, left a smouldering, crushing wreck against the cavern wall. Lane thought, each car he destroyed, what a surface engineering corporation would pay for just one of the gadgets with which those cars were crammed - and he had to destroy the invaluable ancient work to live on, to save anything for future man. He must live. This destroying nemesis behind them must die.

But they had one ace in the hole which Lane was counting on Da Sylva having failed to note. Before leaving their own area, Lane and Saba had posted some thirty men and the remainder of the women in their own master ray chambers. These great beams, which they knew would cover some fifty miles of their route at full extension, constituted a place to run to very definitely. As they neared these caverns which were familiar, near to Eemeeshee's home, Lane sent his telaug beam far ahead, kept screaming a warning to these few remaining stay-at-homes, who were their last resort now. Their children, their women, their homes, and this home-guard ray, were their last hope. As he flashed past an outpost of this small force - one John Flannery, a half-breed Indian of Irish parentage - Lane shouted at him, where he crouched over the ancient mech.

"Give them the works, John, in the fourth passage."

There were four main highways from the north, their flight and attempts at evasion had taken them into the third of these, while Da Sylva had continued with her main force down the fourth, which in the end reached the same goal. Lane had often speculated on the "age" of this fourth passage, which seemed of different and older construction than the other three; was perhaps the first of the many great borings made by the elder race in this area.

Flannery, big red-haired and high-cheek-boned, his blue eyes flashing a reassuring message to John as he flashed past, began at once to fire upon the Da Sylva cars. His great old stationary mech gave off a ray of vastly greater potential of destruction than their own portable weapons, and his solid, unshifting base of rock made his fire more accurate. Lane shot on down the great tube of rock toward the central ray chambers to make sure the force there was made aware of the turn of events.

But there was no need. They had been watching, holding their fire until a sure kill was in order; and at Flannery's attack upon Da Sylva, the vast old central mech began to flame with power, over their heads into the far ways flashed the mighty shafts of death, and within minutes Da Sylva and all her gang were things of the past, smouldering

1333

piles of debris upon the forgotten floors of the Titan's highways.

SABA, taking no chances, ordered at once a return to the Votan caverns. Reduced to a fourth of their original number by the reverses they had suffered, they were not happy as they returned toward Montana's under-rock.

Again at the work of making the former nest of Da Sylva a place safe for themselves, Lane called a meeting of all of the surviving warriors. They stood before him, weary, disheartened at their terrible losses; behind them the ranks of the Votan, ragged, starved wrecks of men; and in their faces the knowledge that they expected of these newcomers only a return to life and perhaps freedom.

Lane realized he had to put heart and hope into these men. He knew the Votans understood English from their long watching of the growing civilization over their heads on the surface; knew, too, that he must not let them return to their old ways of repressive hiding and non-development that had made them easy conquest for Da Sylva's gang.

From these few hundred grim-faced weary men, Lane knew he had to build an organization that would ever after make the wisdom of the caverns safe for future men. He lifted both hands in Indian fashion:

"Men of the Red Race, this struggle seems now to have cost too much. We have paid too highly for what we have won. But that is not true. Nowhere on this dark earth does a band of men exist who have won more for their fellow men with their battle. Nowhere have the dead paid with their lives for more than we have won this day.

The Red Race has won here an opportunity to again become a great world power. Here in this den of lust, here in these forgotten and disregarded caverns, we have paid with our blood for a glorious future for all men. We shall bring modern science into these caverns, studying the ancient science and bringing to us all the value of the wisdom of the glorious race. If we remain as one striving toward a greater and more intelligent organization of red

1334

men everywhere, these ancient machines and rays, coupled with modern science, will give the red man such power and prestige as has not been his since the first Spaniard drew sword in Mexico."

The Votan Indians, listening and realizing that here was a man and a leader different in aims from any they had known, gave forth with a shout of approbation. Lane continued, glad to see in their faces a shining hope that had not been there before.

"You Votans, here in your former homes as our allies and friends, will be not the least pillar of the coming new order in the underworld. As time goes on, and you understand that the ancient ways of vegetating and doing nothing here in these wonder caverns but enjoy the pleasure mech of the Gods and sneer at the poor surface people, are gone; that the modern red man has a greater duty to man on earth and the will to perform that duty. Then you will find yourselves glad to be part of the new Red Legion, a Red Legion using all the mighty science of the Gods for building a new way of life for all men.

## AFTERWORD

THE REST OF this story the future of the world will have to tell. The red men of America are active in the caverns, sometimes ignorant, sometimes backward and too worshipful of the age-old secrecy, but also containing modern men of education and the modern aims of all scientific men everywhere. Even the "creeps" and those people even more changed by the caverns than the creeps, the spider men of the western caverns, are not to be despised because of their knowledge of the wonder world under the rocks of Mother Earth. They will find a way to be useful as civilization comes more and more swiftly to the ancient savage ways of the backward life of the underworld.

The Indians of the underworld are a factor in the coming struggle for power over Earth, and they have a knowledge of the ancient secrets. They have in some areas complete possession of and domination of those mighty mechanisms

1335

of the Elder race. Such battles as the one portrayed are taking place in the west today between the white ray and the red; between modern ray people and those who cling to the ancient tradition of secrecy and suppression of all surface peoples. It seems natural to assume that the red men are on the side of progress, on the side of surface sanity in promoting study and use of the ancient Elder race wisdom for surface men.

For those who seek more knowledge of the Elder world I can tell you the red men know much of it from their legends and from such secret groups as the Red Legion, the Black Legion and others. Whether they will tell you about it is another thing.

The history of the Red Men in the caverns is a fascinating thing. For the next story I am going to select a figure you all think you know, but do you? Apollo. You know all about him. You are wrong. Apollo was a man who came from space, and he came to the American continent in the days when dinosaurs and similar gigantics made life hazardous for the red men. He came for the express purpose of eliminating the serpent race from earth to make way for his own experiments with beneficial rays in making over the race of men on earth toward his ideas of what men should be. That is one reason Apollo has remained as the epitome of masculine beauty the world over. That is what he was: the father of beauty in men. He made it so by moulding men over into his heart's desire. And to do it he held to take the whole world apart. The next story is going to be about Apollo; and it's plenty different from what the school books tell you of this period. They all admit they don't know much about it, don't they. Well, we don't make that mistake. Our guess as to what happened is plenty close - corroborations prove.

Apollo is a mighty figure in Indian legend under many names. He came to the American continent; he wiped out the dinosaurs; he remade the race of men by treating the reproductive portions of their bodies with beneficial rays. By his science he changed the world. Where he came from we don't know, but we know what he did here pretty well. And it doesn't all come from Oahspe. There are many other sources of this view of Apollo.

# THE HIDDEN WORLD
# LETTERS
### FROM THE READERS

Where pertinent information concerning The Shaver Mystery is solicited from those who may have facts of value to offer.

Dear Mr. Palmer:

I am writing you a letter to give you some of my thoughts about the Shaver Mystery. I have not come to any sort of a conclusion about the caverns that are supposed to exist under the surface of the earth as to whether these really exist or not. I think that it is possible for them to exist from the point of view of the belief that the center of the earth is a molten core. I think that the center of the earth may not really be a molten core at all. My personal belief is that it is not. From this point of view the caverns could exist and not be consumed by a very high temperature of heat.

Another question that has occurred in my mind is the problem of air. If the caverns are there and there are inhabitants of these caverns how do they obtain a fresh air supply. This it seems to me they would need because after many thousands of years the supply of air in these caverns would become contaminated even if they are as extensive as Mr. Shaver says that they are. The air shafts then would need to extend to the surface of the earth. But I also think that there would be a requirement for some form of machinery to circulate this air throughout the caverns. Mr. Shaver says that the inhabitants of the caverns have such machinery and that it is imperishable. The weakness to what he says, as I see it, is that machinery as we know it has moving parts, especially machinery used for ventilation purposes. These parts would eventually wear out and require replacement.

Then there is Mr. Shaver's theory that the rays of the sun are dangerous for human beings. There are some people who live in this world who are more constructive than others. Why are not these people equally effected by the sun's rays as those who are more destructive in nature.

Mr. Shaver seems to believe very strongly what he says about the cavern people. To lie about such things would certainly not gain him anything in the world. To use a fiction story to make money from people would be a round about way of doing so. He does not seem to be an individual who is interested only in making money by exploiting the credulity of people. I got the impression that Mr. Shaver is very earnest in his attempt to convince people of the existence of the cavern people. But there are too many things unexplained for the average individual, I believe, to feel that there is enough proof of the existence of these people. Mr. Shaver says that these deros have all sorts of destructive ray at their disposal including various kinds of death ray and also what he calls needle ray which can be used to cut the nerves leading to the mind. If this is true they could have put Mr. Shaver out of commission very quickly if they did not want him to write about them.

As a student of the occult for many years I have read about the sinking of the Continent of Atlantis. Upon such a sinking I would think that those caverns which might be located beneath Atlantis would be flooded with water. All caverns connected with these would also be flooded. If the caverns which were located under Atlantis were connected to those underneath the North American Continent or under the South American Continent, because they were connected, these would also be flooded with water.

I think that Mr. Shaver made a mistake in claiming he was in the caverns if he was not. In the fifth issue of the Hidden World you said that he confidentially told you he had not been in the caverns. This would tend to cause people to doubt other statements he has made or other things that he has written. I also believe that the best way to present a subject is as actual experience or fact not as fiction. All speculations or theories should be labeled as such, not

1338

presented as fact or experience. It is hard enough for people to find truth even in connection with many fairly ordinary subjects of life. With a subject as unusual and as fantastic as this one is, everything should be presented in a strictly truthful way.

To try to separate the various fictional stories that have been presented in the Hidden World, from the various attempts to prove the existence of the cavern people in a more factual manner, is a very difficult task for the average individual, I believe.

Mr. Shaver may have presented personal theories that he has held as fact, because he thought that this would bring people to accept these things sooner. On the contrary this would delay acceptance because in my opinion, the one thing that people are most concerned with is, is a thing true or false.

Perhaps I will write again as I think of other points to question. There are many more things that I could question now but I feel this letter is long enough. I am not signing this letter with my true signature. I wish to remain anonymous. You may publish this letter in the Hidden World if you think it might help some to clarify others ideas about the Shaver Mystery. - A.G., Boston, Mass.

Dear Mr. Shaver:

I have just been reading your Hidden World series, and they have caused me to wonder in a way that may be of interest to you.

I know a man in L.A. that draws pictures, many of them, but of such a nature they are a mystery to everyone. I have taken them to several universities but to no avail. They say, "They are fine works of art but what they mean, we don't know."

This man is not an artist by art standards, because he never had any training but he hears voices and he is guided by these voices, but not the Spiritualist type - no trances. He is told that his voices are from outer space. Another peculiar thing. He does not actually draw pictures. He is a tracer. The picture is projected onto his paper and he traces

1339

the picture. It is simular to what you find in rocks. I never could see anything until he taught me, then the picture is quite visible. Now I see pictures everywhere, but mostly faces of all descriptions.

He also takes old photographs, like in travelog books and traces or rebuilds them into their original form or what we believe to be original. Old buildings he restores, scenery all become alive and meaningful under his hand. The work is truly amazing.

If it were possible I would like you to see these pictures. Maybe they are of the hidden world because no one can interpret them.

Once he was told to draw a picture of his teacher. It came out to be a large brain divided into a left half and a right half, male and female, and within this brain there are hundreds of small minute faces and many other objects, showing what I believe would be memories. I don't know. But a peculiar circumstance occurred. They were on display and we wanted to take a picture of him standing alongside of this teacher picture. All we had was a common box camera. After the picture was developed one half was perfect, the other half was distorted like a double exposure and in the upper corner was half of a flying saucer. How did it get there?

Another time we took some of the pictures to a photographer to have them photographed. They were in a plain wrapping paper envelope. The shop caught fire during the night. The shop was destroyed, even the photographer lost his life as he slept in the building, but the pictures weren't even scorched or wet. They were the only things saved. How come? Isn't this similar to Ray's experience of the flooded basement?

There are still many things we don't understand and this is one of them. I would like to hear from you if you are interested. Maybe you have the key. - Jack Campbell D.C., California Hot Springs, California.

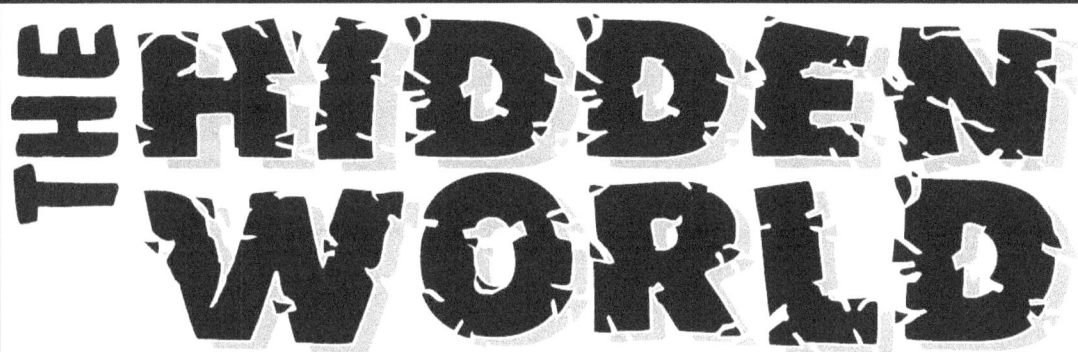

**HERE NOW ARE** the first TWO VOLUMES in a continuing series originally released by Publisher Ray Palmer in the 1960s, and hereby reprinted for the Serious Student of the Shaver and Inner Earth Mysteries!

**TO COME IN TOTAL 16 BOOKS, OVER 3200 PAGES AND ALMOST TWO MILLION WORDS!
14 MORE VOLUMES TO COME!**

**HIDDEN WORLD NUMBER ONE:**
**The Dero! The Tero! And The Battle For Good And Evil Underground!**

Here, in over 200 pages, is the beginning of The Shaver Mystery!

· Shaver hears the tormented voices coming from below.

· Readers question his sanity when he describes entering the caves of the ancients.

· He describes in detail the plunder of our planet by extraterrestrials in ancient times, and the lost continents of Lemuria and Atlantis.

· Shaver "proves his case" by revealing an ancient alphabet he calls "Mantong."

· Captured by the Dero from ancient races, the stem and mech machines cause utter chaos on surface dwellers, Wars, murder and horrific accidents are caused by the "evil ones."

**THIS RARE REPRINT ONLY $25.00**

**HIDDEN WORLD NUMBER TWO:**
**The Masked World of Richard Shaver**

The epic underground saga continues in roughly 190 pages of the nightmarish dealings with Inner Earth dwellers.

· A dark cloud hangs over the Earth as the subsurface mutants kidnap and torture humans, even performing cannibalistic acts upon their flesh.

· A series of airplane crashes carrying well-known celebrities can be blamed on the demented robot-like Dero.

· Shave reveals the secrets of "Growing A Better Man."

· Voices in the night torment readers of Shaver's tales as they confirm many of his claims.

**THIS RARE REPRINT ONLY $25.00**

**SPECIAL OFFER: Both volumes One and Two of THE HIDDEN WORLD for the combined price of just $39.95. Please add $5.00 S/H to the total order.**

**Explore The Shaver and Inner Earth Mysteries**

**Global Communications**
**Box 753 · New Brunswick, NJ 08903**

# THE HIDDEN WORLD

Free DVD On Inner Earth When You Purchase Any Three Items From This Advertisement.

## RESEARCH AND BOOKS ON THE INNER EARTH, HOLLOW GLOBE AND SHAVER MYSTERIES

❏ The Smokey God and Other Inner Earth Mysteries—A voyage inside the earth and the truth about UFOs from Inner Earth and Telos, by Olaf Johnson, with Ray Palmer and Shurula—$15.00

❏ Etidorpha—Journet to Another Land. "Official Edition." 150-year-old classic. Secret Society member enters a cave in Kentucky to begin his strange journey—$25.00

❏ Subterranean Worlds Inside Earth by Timothy Green Beckley. Explores the Shaver Mystery and unexplained subterranean world tales—$15.00

❏ Richard Shaver and the Reality of The Inner Earth by Tim Swartz. Previous unpublished works with free audio CD—$25.00

❏ The Secret World—Rare hardcover classic with Ray Palmer and Richard Shaver, featuring his "rock book" paintings, with audio interview of Shaver and Palmer—$32.00

❏ Messages From The Hollow Earth by Dianne Robbins. Masters of Telos speak—$20.00

❏ Telos: The Call Goes Out From The Hollow Earth and the Underground Cities by Dianne Robbins—$18.95

❏ The Phantom of the Poles by William Reed— A rare classic long sought by collectors—$18.00

Please add $5.00 for each book or every two books for S/H

❏ Lost Worlds and Underground Mysteries of the Far East by M. Paul Dare—$18.00

❏ The Arctic Home in the Vedas by Lokomanya Bai Gangadhar Tilak. Rare Indian manuscript describes Inner Earth—$23.95

❏ Quest For Inner Earth by Dorothy Leon—$17.95

❏ Twilight: Hidden Chambers Beneath The Earth by T. Lobsang Rampa—$22.00

❏ Dweller On Two Planets by Philos The Tibetan. Early Mt. Shasta contacts—$19.95

❏ Incredible Cities of Inner Earth by David H. Lewis. Written in stunning, novel-like form, but all too true!—$21.95

❏ Mysteries of the Pyramid by David H. Lewis. Secret chambers revealed—$21.95

❏ Admiral Byrd's Secret Journal Beyond The Poles by Tim Swartz. Here is the untold, inside story, of a vayage beyond belief!—$22.00

❏ Caverns, Cauldrons, and Concealed Creatures, Expanded 2nd Edition! by Mike Mott. Thick book with color plates. Subsurface myths, legends and reality—$29.95

❏ Finding Lost Atlantis Inside The Hollow Earth. Rare reprint by Brinsley Le Por Trench. British Royalty gives excellent references—$22.00

❏ Missing Diary of Admiral Richard E. Byrd. Rare text, lost for years, now as a reprint—$15.00

**Global Communications • Box 753-TGS
New Brunswick, NJ 08903**

Credit card customers use our secure 24-hour hotline at 732-602-3407 — All major cards.
PayPal at MrUFO8@hotmail.com